THE MARSHALL CAVENDISH
☆ ☆ ☆ ILLUSTRATED ☆ ☆ ☆
ENCYCLOPEDIA OF
WORLD WAR II

VOLUME 4

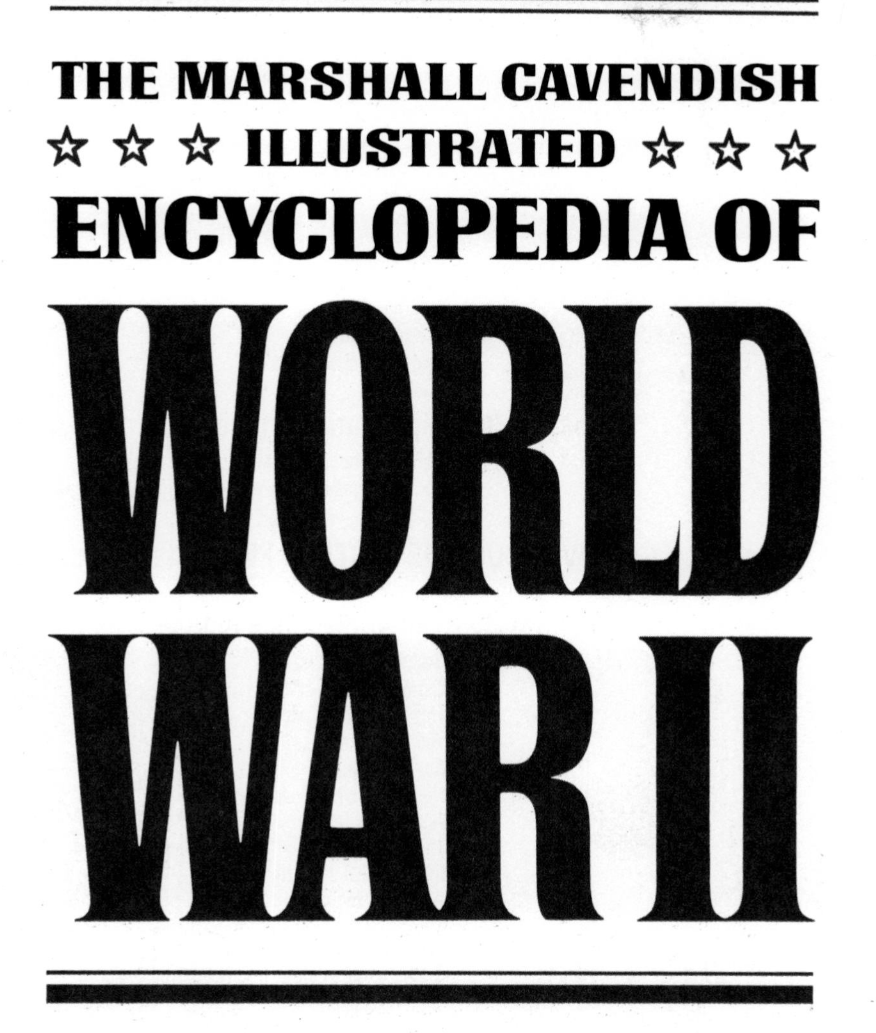

Based on the original text by
Lieutenant Colonel Eddy Bauer

CONSULTANT EDITOR

Brigadier General James L. Collins, Jr., U.S.A.

CHIEF OF MILITARY HISTORY,
DEPARTMENT OF THE ARMY

MARSHALL CAVENDISH CORPORATION/NEW YORK

CONTENTS

Editorial Director: Brian Innes
Editor-in-chief; Brigadier Peter Young, D.S.O., M.C., M.A.
Managing Editor: Richard Humble
Editor: Christopher Chant
Art Editor: Jim Bridge

Library of Congress Catalog No. 72-95429
Printed in Great Britain

The coming of
GLOBAL WAR

CHAPTER 32

The War transformed

Δ Red Army troops attack during one of the murderous battles on the Eastern Front which transformed the whole conduct–and outcome–of the war.

In 1941 the war which had been confined mainly to Europe since September 1939 really became a world war.

In the summer and autumn of 1940, German warships had cruised in the South Atlantic, the Indian Ocean, the Pacific, and even as far as the Antarctic ice barrier. But irritating as these pinpricks were, their strategic effect was virtually nil; the German Navy could not make much play with its naval forces even in home waters, and in this war against mercantile tonnage the British Home Fleet did not bother with them as long as they kept clear of the British convoys.

But when Hitler invaded Russia on June 22, 1941, the war spread from the German-Soviet demarcation line drawn across Poland in September 1939 to Vladivistok and the Bering Strait. In December 1941 Japan's entry into the war extended the war by land, sea, and air across the enormous area stretching from east to west between the Hawaiian Islands and Ceylon, and from north to south between the Aleutian Islands and Guadalcanal. The war now became a direct sequel to the apparently endless war between China and Japan, which had been in progress since 1932. From 1941 this series of bitter hostilities can be called "World War II" in every sense of the term.

With the entry into the war of the United States and the Soviet Union, both of them industrial giants, the material and technical aspects of the war now became more significant. Obviously, not all the battles after 1941 were decided beforehand in the factories and the research laboratories. But it is certainly true to say that from 1941 every belligerent state was run on a war economy and an increasing mobilisation of industry, as is reflected by the continually rising production of every type of armament in Germany, Great Britain, the United States, and the Soviet Union.

But the figures need close examination. In Germany, tank production increased twelve-fold (from 2,235 to 27,345 tanks) between 1941 and 1944; the Pzkw I and II ($5\frac{3}{4}$ and $10\frac{1}{4}$ tons respectively) ceased production and were replaced by the Pzkw V – the Panther, 45 tons – and the Pzkw VI – the Tiger, 56 tons. American aircraft production underwent an even greater increase. In 1941, 317 four-engined bombers came off the assembly lines; in 1943 and 1944, 25,946 were built, including

about 4,000 Boeing B-29 Superfortresses. Clearly Germany and Japan, as well as Italy, could not match America and the Soviet Union in industrial capacity, and the consequences of this state of affairs dominated the war after 1941.

Axis world strategy

Firstly, Hitler, confronted by the Soviet Union, and Tojo, confronted by the U.S.A., would have to act quickly and strike a succession of devastating and decisive blows at their enemies; they could not permit the latter to recover from their first surprise and eventually bring their undoubted material superiority into play. Having decided to attack, Germany and Japan were therefore each compelled to adopt a bold strategy.

Secondly, the main objective of their war policy – originally defined by Clausewitz as the destruction of the enemy's organised armed forces – was now governed by the need to obtain strategic raw materials. In geographical terms this meant coal from the Donets basin, iron ore from Krivoy Rog, manganese from Nikopol, nickel from Petsamo, oil from the Caucasus, the Dutch East Indies, and Burma, and rubber from the Malay States. Hitler used this economic argument freely to justify his most daring and even his most absurd decisions to his generals. In any event, after June 22, 1941, Germany's entire strategy had to take these factors into account, although resources of all kinds had been made available by the victories of 1939 and 1940, and although commercial treaties had been concluded with satellite and neutral countries as a result of those victories.

For the same reasons, communications across the sea between Britain and America became of vital importance. It was essential for these two powers to be able to intercept raiders and to protect their communications by land and sea. From the time of Pearl Harbor – and even before, as far as Great Britain was concerned – the United States undoubtedly held the position of the "great arsenal of democracy". The consequences would have been serious if a half, or even a third, of the cargoes of arms and equipment from American factories had been sunk in the Atlantic or the Pacific. Fortunately for the Allies, over four

△ *Illustration from the German magazine* Signal *shows how the Third Reich's propagandists justified the invasion of Soviet Russia: a European crusade against Bolshevism.*

million tons of material, including 5,000 tanks and over 7,000 aircraft, reached the Soviet Union from Britain and America via Murmansk and Archangel – a task requiring the convoying of 720 merchantmen and tankers.

In the latter half of 1940 Hitler and Göring were completely mistaken about the results to be expected from the Luftwaffe's night bombing offensive against the sources of Britain's war production. Equally so, Churchill and the Chief of Air Staff, Sir Charles Portal, were just as misguided about the damage which Bomber Command could do to Germany's war industries. In 1941 the destruction so wrought was negligible, and even at the beginning of 1943 it was hardly perceptible. From the summer of 1943, however, the British bombers did begin to make themselves felt, but even then they did not seriously curtail the production of German tanks and aircraft, which reached record heights in 1944.

The Third Reich's attack on the Soviet Union introduced into the war a new element which was at least as important as the others we have mentioned.

World War II had had a particularly ideological aspect right from its beginning, a factor which had been entirely lacking in World War I. The dictator states, headed by Hitler and Mussolini, were opposed by the democratic and parliamentarian states of central and western Europe. But the ideological character of the war became far more pronounced after the German invasion of Russia on June 22, 1941. From that day two equally totalitarian states, two international organisations, (one might almost say two religions), faced each other on the battlefield.

Each of the two adversaries was fighting not only enemies but heretics on the Eastern Front: "German Fascists", according to the jargon used in Moscow, and "Jew Bolsheviks", as denounced by Hitler, Goebbels, and the Nazi propaganda machine. It was therefore not surprising that in these circumstances the German-Soviet war did not conform with the rules for belligerents laid down by international law and the Geneva Convention.

Hitler's order, issued before the outbreak of hostilities, to shoot the political commissars appointed by Moscow is well known. But there is no doubt that criminal directives of the same kind were also given by the Russians on their side of the front. The best evidence for this is the high mortality rate – around 85 per cent – of German, Italian, and Japanese prisoners-of-war in Soviet camps.

The German-Soviet war, like the Wars of Religion in the 16th and 17th Centuries, transcended the bounds of nationality. In this respect Hitler was less fortunate than Stalin. His European "crusade against Bolshevism" commanded only scanty support in France, Belgium, Holland, Denmark, and Norway; most of the volunteers from these countries were enlisted by the *Waffen-S.S.* in 1941. Stalin, on the other hand, right from the beginning of the war, commanded the unconditional and unlimited support of all the European Communist parties; these soon became the well-disciplined allies of the resistance movements which had been organised in the occupied countries, although they remained separate, cohesive bodies and retained their party slogans.

Another aspect of the ideological side of the war is rarely mentioned and deserves brief notice. From 1941 onwards, Soviet espionage had the necessary facilities for infiltrating its agents into Britain and America. It appears to have escaped general attention that the great treason trials in Britain and the United States during the period 1945–50 had their origins in the years when Stalin, Roosevelt, and Churchill were being photographed in apparent harmony during their meetings. The "anti-Fascist" mystique cultivated in Moscow, London, and Washington had an enormous attraction for some British and American citizens, both native and naturalised, and they therefore thought they were entitled to abandon the loyalty which bound them to their countries.

This is not to say that Roosevelt and Churchill ignored security precautions when they pledged their alliance to the Soviet Union in 1941. They would certainly have been acutely embarrassed if they had suspected the sinister facts: the Soviet missions which, in accordance with the Lend-Lease agreement, were requesting arms, munitions, fuel, raw materials, and food, were also engaged in secret recruiting and Intelligence work, in the belief that a third world war would immediately follow the downfall of Hitler and Mussolini.

Such excuses can reasonably be advanced only for the first two years of the tripartite alliance, which Churchill, thinking of the wars against Louis XIV, refers to in *The Second World War* as the "Grand Alliance". After the summer of 1943, however, the Allies' negligence became inexcusable.

△ *Hitler crying for the moon–the invasion of Britain–as seen by London's* Punch. *"Do not underestimate England," Churchill had said to Ribbentrop in 1937. Ribbentrop, then German Ambassador to Britain, had shrugged off the warning contemptuously. Certainly Hitler had got into his head the idea that "Our enemies are little worms; I saw them at Munich." And he never grasped the true meaning of Britain's determination to fight on. Like Napoleon before him he chose to bury his head in the sand, and declined to modify his policies so that Germany's war aims could be pursued with British resistance being taken into account.*

Hitler: eternal enigma

Hitler's personality, naturally enough, played a dominant rôle in framing the events of 1941. Since the end of World War II his reputation as a modern Caligula or Nero, universally condemned as a monstrous criminal, has never been seriously challenged. But no generals or politicians of his former entourage have ever reached objective agreement about the Führer's ability as a military commander; and this deserves some study.

At the Nuremberg war crime trials after the war, Keitel and Jodl both described Hitler's strategic intuition, his prodigious memory, his precise knowledge of the

HITLER
SUPREME WARLORD

Autocrat of Germany, Supreme Commander of the Wehrmacht, overlord of Europe–such was Hitler's position as 1941 opened. The power of the German Führer had never been greater.
1. *Head of state: Hitler with Prince Paul, Regent of Yugoslavia, in 1939.* **2.** *The naïve vulgarity of Nazi taste–a painting in the* Führerhaus *in Munich.*
3. *The cult of the Führer: a miniature of Hitler found on an S.S. man.* **4.** *The founding father of the "Greater Germany" created by the Third Reich–Hitler during the 1938 "electoral campaign" in Graz, Austria.* **5.** *Hitler's desk in the New Chancellery, Berlin, the scene of many a surrender to the growth of Nazi Germany.* **6.** *"Führer and Supreme Commander of the Wehrmacht" by Conrad Hommel.*

most insignificant details of military history and technology, and his quickness in understanding the problems of the art of war. Rundstedt, on the other hand, once referred to him in private as a "Bohemian corporal", and since 1945 many leading generals have written memoirs which dwell at length on Hitler's political and strategic errors. But after the French armistice Hitler's sycophantic staff referred to him as "*Der grösste Feldherr aller Zeiten*" (the greatest general of all time).

Soviet historians regard this type of criticism of Hitler's errors, which is made with certain modifications by nearly all German generals, as a puerile attempt to conceal their own responsibility and to minimise their own mistakes in the conduct of the war. These generals tend to represent Hitler as the sole scapegoat for the sins of the German people in general and for those of the German General Staff in particular.

Clearly it would be absurd to put blind faith in all the stories about Hitler retailed by German writers; it would also be just as absurd to make Hitler alone responsible for the successive defeats which precipitated the final collapse of the Third Reich. It had already been pointed out that Rundstedt was as least as much to blame as Hitler for the issuing of the order on May 24, 1940, directing the Panzers to halt outside Dunkirk, thereby letting the B.E.F. re-embark for England.

But in fact these critics were not all influenced by Germany's defeat in 1945; nor were they relying on the fact that Hitler, Göring, Keitel, and Jodl were no longer alive to contradict their statements. A classic example can be found in the diaries kept by General Halder daily up to September 24, 1942, which have already been quoted on the subject of the campaign in France.

The following comment on the supreme master of the Third Reich's strategy dates from July 23, 1942, when Field-Marshal List's army group was approaching Rostov, the gateway to the Caucasus. "[Hitler's] continual under-estimation of the moves at the enemy's disposal is more and more grotesque, and is becoming dangerous. The position is now getting quite intolerable. It is no longer possible to get any serious work done. Hitler's idea of 'conducting operations' is to follow neurotic reactions based on momentary impressions and to show a total inability to appreciate the apparatus of command."

Certainly Hitler had a kind of intuitive grasp of the principles of warfare. This was strengthened by his reading of Frederick the Great, Clausewitz, Moltke, and Schlieffen. He had met Ludendorff and had discussed military problems with him; and Hitler's formidable talents were sustained by his belief in his mission, his implacable will-power, and his total lack of scruples and human feelings.

Unquestionably, the strategic conception behind the German victories of 1940 was Hitler's work. There was the daring shown in the decision to make five simultaneous landings in Norway, in the face of the Royal Navy's enormous superiority; and it will also be recalled how readily Hitler responded to Manstein's strategic plans for the attack on the West, and how quickly he assimilated them and made them his own. Hitler also conceived

▽ *Hitler visits his troops. At the time of the invasion of Soviet Russia in June 1941 his hold over the Army High Command was stronger than ever before. And the respect in which he was held by the rank and file was strengthened by his as yet unbroken record of success.*

the idea of sailing the battle-cruisers *Scharnhorst* and *Gneisenau* through the Channel in daylight in February 1942.

Napoleon claimed that when he worked out a plan of campaign he experienced all the labour-pains of a woman giving birth to a child, but that as soon as the campaign began he was always imperturbable and determined, with eyes and ears open, ready to take immediate decisions. Hitler certainly seemed to initiate his plans with the sureness of a sleep-walker (to whom he sometimes compared himself); but he tended to lack audacity when carrying out his plans. In fact he did not have the supreme quality of a military commander which Napoleon, who had it to a supreme degree, once called "courage at two o'clock in the morning".

For example, when Hitler heard that Commodore Bonte's destroyer flotilla had been destroyed at Narvik, he lost all self-control and wanted to order General Dietl to withdraw across the Swedish frontier with his men. A few weeks later, when the French campaign had begun, he kept interfering with the working of O.K.H., as he was terrified of a powerful counter-attack against Sedan from the direction of Rethel, although all Intelligence clearly showed that this assumption was absurd.

To sum up, Hitler was unsure of himself, indecisive, finicky, shuffling, and hesitant in execution, sticking obstinately to any thoughtless decision, and he was all the more sour and morose when he had hesitated a long time before taking such a decision. Moreover, as he had not been trained as a staff officer he was quite incapable, for all his undeniable strategic talents, of co-ordinating his operations according to a timed plan, or of adjusting his objectives to suit the resources available to him.

For this he was compelled to turn to his highly-qualified subordinates in the Armed Forces High Command (O.K.W.), and particularly in the Army High Command (O.K.H.). In addition, quite apart from his general mistrust of all and sundry, Hitler seems to have had the same aversion to staff officers that was shown many British, French, and German front-line soldiers in World War I.

With regard to his generals, Hitler undoubtedly had the situation better in hand in 1941 than in the first quarter of 1940. The Norwegian and French campaigns had clearly shown that those generals who had predicted defeat or even catastrophe if the Wehrmacht should be so ill advised as to move forward from the Siegfried Line had been completely mistaken. The atmosphere of dissension which had been spread by Blaskowitz, Witzleben, and Leeb had now been dissipated. Those who had had doubts in the previous winter, such as Brauchitsch and Halder, did not accept the basic principles of the régime, but they obeyed Hitler's directives more submissively than before. And Hitler, with his prestige enhanced by his victories, was now in a position to smash all opposition.

Many German generals, both at the

▵ *Typical of the Soviet reply to the German invasion: "We shall not give up the gains of October!" –referring to the Bolshevik Revolution of 1917 and its subsequent achievements. One of the most striking characteristics of the Russo-German war was this fundamental, head-on collision between the two greatest totalitarian states in the world.*

Nuremberg trials and in their memoirs, claimed that they had been stunned when they heard of Hitler's decision to attack the Soviet Union. But none of the documents relating to that decision reveal any opposition in principle within the German Army High Command to the venture. Hitler therefore imposed his will on everyone, and undoubtedly the enormous successes which he more or less forced on his generals made him even less ready to listen to their arguments.

In any event, the German Army remained poised for instant action on any front during the interval between the postponement of the invasion of England and Rommel's arrival in Libya. This alone suggests that, during the period in question, friction between the Supreme Commander of the German Armed Forces and the Army High Command was infrequent. Hitler exercised his authority by issuing general directives, and the Army High Command then converted them into plans for troop concentrations or operational orders with its customary efficiency and promptness.

Hitler, supreme warlord

But after the invasion of Russia in June 1941 there was renewed friction with O.K.H., and this led Hitler to take over command of the Army from Brauchitsch.

From then onwards the former Bavarian Army corporal combined in his own person the offices of Head of State (Führer), Chief of Government (Chancellor), Supreme Commander of the Armed Forces (O.K.W.), and Supreme Commander of the Army (O.K.H.). We should also bear in mind that he still retained his post as leader of the National Socialist Party. Thus Hitler combined in his own person a concentration of powers such as Ludendorff had recommended to the German people in his book *Total War* in 1936.

There was, therefore, no way in which Hitler could be relieved of his command, in the way that the younger Moltke had been by the Kaiser after the Battle of the Marne and Falkenhayn after Verdun. Nor had he any political superior whom the General Staff might persuade to replace him, as had happened to Bethmann-Hollweg in 1917. Nor, in the end, could Hitler find himself in the position of the Kaiser, driven to abdicate when the Chancellor and the General Staff had combined against him. Hitler, as it were, was Kaiser, Chancellor, and Chief of the General Staff, as though empowered to sign his directives "By Order of his Majesty the Kaiser".

It is also clearly doubtful whether or not Hitler was physically and intellectually capable of bearing his great responsibilities. There is much evidence to suggest that as early as 1944 he had no purpose or energy left. General Frido von Senger und Etterlin, who received the Oak Leaves to the Knight's Cross from Hitler after his successful defensive battle at Monte Cassino, gave the following description of the Führer in 1944:

"The ceremony for those who were to be honoured was far from impressive. Hitler made a really horrifying impression, and in spite of myself I wondered how the young officers and sergeants who were being decorated with me would react . . . . . . His unattractive figure, with his short neck, appeared more slovenly than ever. The skin of his face was flaccid, his complexion pale and creased by lack of sleep. The look in his blue eyes, which was said to have completely fascinated so many people, was vacant, possibly as a result of the stimulants which he was continually given. His handshake was floppy. His left arm hung limp and trembling . . ."

It is not clear whether this was the result of illness or of the absurd diet to which Hitler kept. According to information that reached Switzerland in 1943 Hitler may have suffered from Parkinson's Disease; this would to some extent account for the trembling of his left hand, which had been noted by Senger und Etterlin and others before the bomb plot of July 20, 1944. Some writers have suggested that Hitler was an epileptic. Because of the secrecy in which the Führer's health was always shrouded a definite diagnosis is almost impossible. What is quite certain is that in 1939 Hitler used his excellent health as an argument against the advisers who would have preferred to postpone the launching of a war until 1945 or 1946. As Hitler had just celebrated his 50th birthday, it is possible that Hitler already felt that he was rapidly approaching a period of complete physical degeneration.

It is also certain that nobody could have endured a way of life like Hitler's for very long. After dealing with military matters in long sessions and allowing his generals to make little more than monosyllabic comments, he spent the night until 2 or 3 o'clock in the morning in haranguing his

▽ Hitler with his personal physician, Dr. Morell–an unsavoury quack whose wide-ranging prescription of drugs was instrumental in bringing forward Hitler's physical decline.

Party colleagues. (The shorthand record of his statements, made on the orders of Martin Bormann, makes up a large volume of ferocious and redundant banalities.) Then a few hours of sleep, a boiling hot bath, and Hitler was ready to hold forth again without pause as he studied the war situation map which had been brought up to date overnight.

Hitler relied upon Doctor Morell, who was regarded by his professional colleagues as a dangerous quack, to keep up his strength from one day to the next. This dubious figure gave his patient a good dose of sleeping pills after his exertions of the night; early in the morning Hitler was also given a strychnine injection which helped to revive him, and later a few benzedrine pills.

In any event this mental and physical decline was only just beginning in 1941. According to Halder's personal diary and the O.K.H. War Diary, Hitler was still extremely active, completely self-confident, and able to make everyone do exactly what he wanted. But these same documents also show clearly that he used to avoid an issue when a strategic decision was essential. In his relations with his generals Hitler used an ingenious deceptive technique: sometimes, when he had a favourable opportunity, he would turn the discussion on to subjects with which they were unfamiliar; at other times he would switch their attention to points of detail or historical analogies, where his amazing memory put him in full control of the situation.

△ *July 19, 1940: Hitler and his newly-promoted marshals.* Left to right: *Keitel, Rundstedt, Bock, and Göring; Brauchitsch, Leeb, List, Kluge, Witzleben, and Reichenau. Like Napoleon and the first French marshals created in 1804, Hitler's choice for the marshal's baton ranged from close adherents of the régime, like Keitel and Göring, to hard-bitten professionals such as Rundstedt and Bock.*

CHAPTER 33

Enter Rommel

For 18 months, between March 1941 and September 1942, Erwin Rommel displayed outstanding ability to attack and to manoeuvre, learning to combine cunning with force. There is no doubt that the man who managed to rebound from a decisive defeat before Tobruk into an advance which took him to the gates of Alexandria must be counted among the truly great commanders of all time.

But was his brilliance as a tactician matched by his strategic ability? This is not so clear. One firm criterion of sound strategy is that it must combine the different interests of land, sea, and air forces into a framework which Churchill described with the ugly word "triphibian". And Rommel repeatedly failed to do this.

During the summer of 1942, for example, Rommel constantly blamed *Comando Supremo* for the frequent breakdowns in his supply system, forgetting that after taking Tobruk on June 21 he had assured Cavallero that he would be able to reach the Nile with the help of the fuel and transport captured in Tobruk. He also forgot that although he was keeping Luftwaffe squadrons from the task of neutralising Malta, the British bombers, torpedo-bombers, and submarines based on the island were exacting a merciless toll on the Italian merchant tonnage in the central Mediterranean. In fact, it was on Rommel's urgent request – despite the protests of Kesselring and Cavallero – that Hitler and Mussolini gave up Operation "Hercules", which could and should have presented the Axis with Malta and Gozo.

Whatever one may think of Rommel in a historical context, his former subordinates and opponents all pay tribute to his nobility of character and his high moral code. Undoubtedly his task in fighting a "clean war" in the African desert was easier than that of his colleagues on the Eastern Front, who had the partisans and Hitler to deal with. But when slight scuffles broke out between his troops and Arab tribesmen, whom British agents were trying to enlist against the Italians, Rommel noted in his diary on September 16, 1942: "There is nothing so unpleasant as partisan warfare. It is perhaps very important not to make reprisals on hostages at the first outbreak of partisan warfare, for these only create feelings of revenge and serve to strengthen the *franc-tireurs*. It is better to allow an incident to go unavenged than to hit back at the innocent. It only agitates the whole neighbourhood, and hostages easily become martyrs."

In 1944 Rommel protested to Hitler in the same spirit of humanity, good sense, and true German patriotism against the appalling massacre of French civilians at Oradour-sur-Glane perpetrated by the S.S. *Das Reich* Panzer Division, and demanded exemplary punishment for those responsible for the crime. (The result was a coarse and violent rebuff.) The honourable treatment which Rommel offered to the Free French prisoners taken at Bir

◁ *Erwin Rommel, the "Desert Fox"* (left) *tours the front with his staff officers.*

▽ *New factor in the Desert War–* Afrika Korps *Panzer units move up to the front on the* Via Balbia–*the lifeline along the Libyan coast which the Italians built before the war.*

△ *Help for the Italians:* Afrika Korps *armour reaches the quayside at Tripoli. In the light of Rommel's later spectacular successes it is often hard to remember that the original purpose of the German desert army was nothing more than the defence of the Libyan capital.*
▷ *Air cover for Rommel–the Luftwaffe arrives in North Africa to support the* Afrika Korps. *A* Schwarm *of Messerschmitt 109 fighters takes off* (above), *and Junkers 52 transports bring in supplies and fuel for an advance air base in the open desert.*

Hakeim in June 1942 should also be noted. It ignored the fact that the Franco-German armistice of 1940, according to the rules and usages of war, had deprived de Gaulle's Free French adherents of the status and privileges of regular combatants.

Rommel was also an attentive husband, who wrote to his wife every day to keep her in touch with his fortunes. The following extracts come from two successive letters (the second contains a thinly-veiled reference to his new assignment in Africa).

"February 6, 1941

"Dearest Lu,

"Landed at Staaken 12.45. First to C.in-C. Army, who appointed me to my new job, and then to Führer. Things are moving fast. My kit is coming on here. I can only take barest necessities with me. Perhaps I'll be able to get the rest out soon. I need not tell you that my head is swimming with all the many things there are to be done. It'll be months before anything materialises.

"So 'our leave' was cut short again. Don't be sad, it had to be. The new job is very big and important."

"February 7, 1941.

"Slept on my new job last night. It's one way of getting my rheumatism treatment. I've got a lot to do, in the few hours that remain, getting together all I need."

This was typical of Rommel. And one can only conclude that when his widow and his son, Manfred, chose the title *War Without Hate* for the collection of letters and memoirs which he left, it was a perfectly appropriate decision.

The British and the Greeks

While the advance units of the *Afrika Korps* were leaving Italy for Africa General Wavell in Cairo was carrying out the orders he had received from London. The 6th Australian Division, the 2nd New Zealand Division (Major-General B. C. Freyberg) and over half the 2nd Armoured Division (Major-General M. D. Gambier-Parry), which had just arrived from England, were to be sent to help the Greeks.

Brigadier E. Dorman-Smith, an officer of G.H.Q. Middle East in Cairo, who had been at the front with O'Connor from Mechili to Beda Fomm, returned to Cairo to see Wavell at 1000 hours on February 12 (a few hours, in fact, before Rommel called on Gariboldi in Tripoli), and heard about this new change of front from Wavell, Dorman-Smith remarked that while he had been away from G.H.Q. the usual maps of the Western Desert on the walls had been replaced by maps of Greece, and that Wavell commented sardonically: "You see, Eric, I'm starting my spring campaign."

On the previous day Wavell had in fact cabled Churchill after receiving a message from Lieutenant-General Sir Henry Maitland Wilson in Tobruk, informing him that the Italian forces were in a state

of collapse. At the front, O'Connor stated that he was ready to move forward into Tripolitania if all available troops were sent to reinforce his 7th Armoured Division, and if the R.A.F. and Admiral Cunningham's Inshore Squadron (one monitor and three gunboats) could harrass the Italian-held coastline and give him the necessary support. On the latter assumption he had planned amphibious operations against Buerat and subsequently against Misurata, further along the coast.

O'Connor's optimism was matched in Tripoli by Rommel's initial pessimism. The latter had just received a discouraging report from Lieutenant Heggenreiner, a German liaison officer in North Africa. Rommel noted that Heggenreiner "described some very unpleasant incidents which had occurred during the retreat, or rather the rout which it had become. Italian troops had thrown away their weapons and ammunition and clambered on to overloaded vehicles in a wild attempt to get away to the west. This had led to some ugly scenes, and even to shooting. Morale was as low as it could be in all military circles in Tripoli. Most of the Italian officers had already packed their bags and were hoping for a quick return trip to Italy."

General Gariboldi now had only five divisions under his orders: the "Bologna", "Brescia", "Pavia", "Sabratha", and "Savona" Divisions. Even on June 10, 1940, these had been considered "ineffi-

▵ Rommel's desert flank: an oasis reconnaissance force.
▹ The left-hand prong of Rommel's triple advance was the thrust along the coast road to Benghazi. This tank belongs to Rommel's principal unit in his first desert offensive–General Streich's 5th Light Division.

cient" and had since had to give up part of their equipment to the recently-destroyed 10th Army. But for the formal orders of the British War Cabinet, nothing could have kept O'Connor and the victors of Sidi Barrani, Bardia, Tobruk, Mechili, and Beda Fomm from driving through to Tripoli.

But Churchill had already made his decision, and it was adhered to. For once Sir John Dill, the C.I.G.S., supported the Prime Minister's view. But Brooke, still C.-in-C., Home Forces, believed that Churchill's decision overreached the possibilities of British strategy, considering the means then available. Brooke later wrote: "This is one of the very few occasions on which I doubted Dill's advice and judgement, and I am not in a position to form any definite opinion as I was not familiar with all the facts. I have, however, always considered from the very start that our participation in the operations in Greece was a definite strategic blunder. Our hands were more than full at that time in the Middle East, and Greece could only result in the most dangerous dispersal of force."

Brooke's fears were certainly proved correct by the course of events. But the British felt themselves bound to go to the aid of the Greeks, quite apart from the fact that a refusal to do so would have been a gift for the Axis propagandists. There was always the possibility that without British help the Greeks might have been tempted to negotiate some arrangement with Hitler. On the other hand, the sending of a British expeditionary force to Greece proved to the world that Britain was not pursuing a policy of national self-interest. Despite the defeats in Greece and Crete, the attempt did much to save British prestige – more so than if it had not been made. The same cannot be said for projects such as Operation "Mandible", which compelled Wavell to keep the 7th Australian Division in the Nile Delta for a possible attack on Rhodes and Leros.

The desert front

As G.H.Q. Cairo was forced to give up the troops for this expeditionary force, it was left with only skeleton forces to "consolidate" its position in western Cyrenaica, according to orders. These forces consisted mainly of the rump of the 2nd

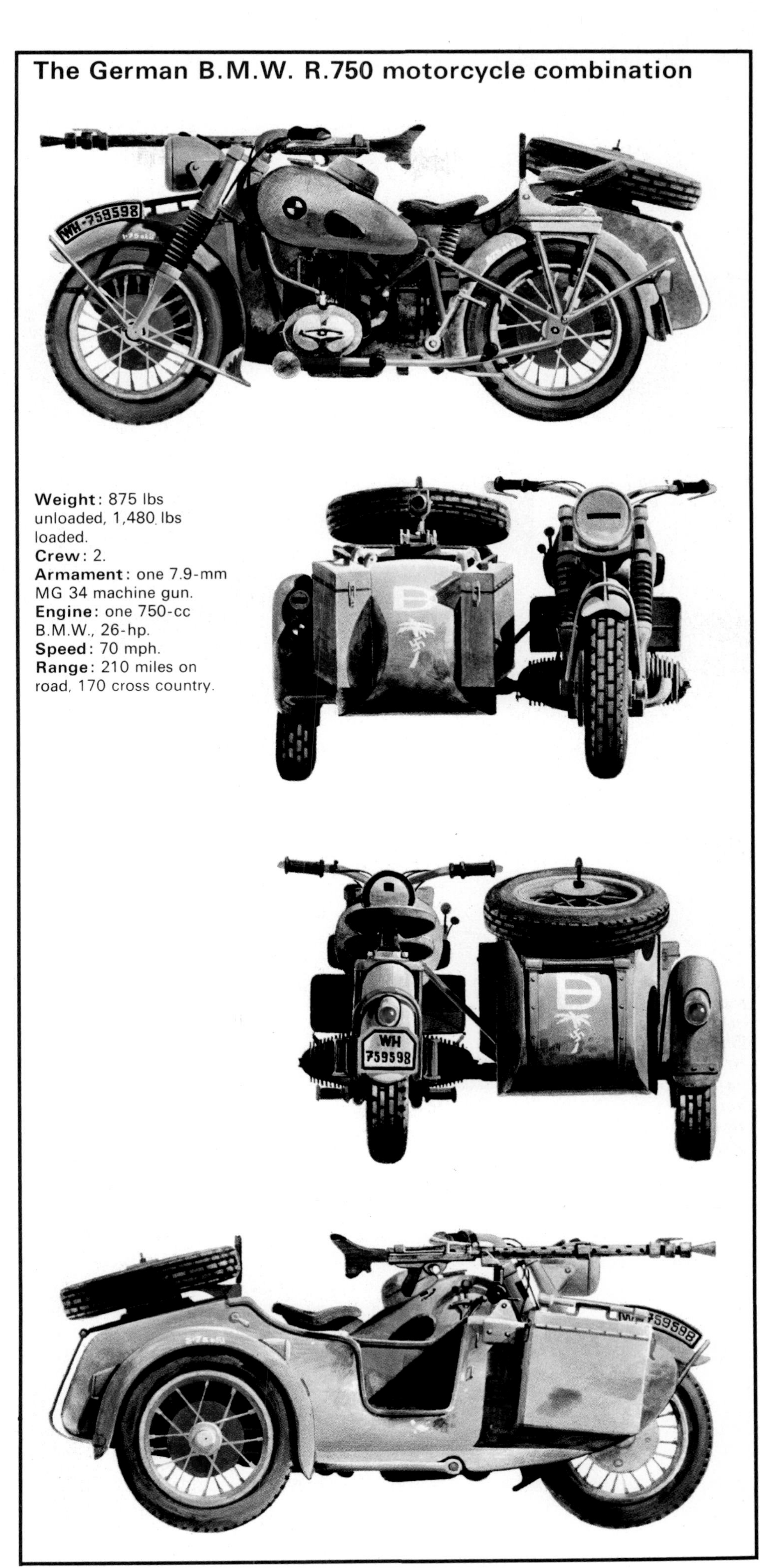

The German B.M.W. R.750 motorcycle combination

Weight: 875 lbs unloaded, 1,480 lbs loaded.
Crew: 2.
Armament: one 7.9-mm MG 34 machine gun.
Engine: one 750-cc B.M.W., 26-hp.
Speed: 70 mph.
Range: 210 miles on road, 170 cross country.

▵ Afrika Korps *artillery in action. In a later note on the rules of desert warfare, Rommel wrote: "The artillery must have great range and must, above all, be capable of great mobility and of carrying with it ammunition in large quantities." Here, however, the* Afrika Korps *was at a disadvantage. General Fritz Bayerlein, who in time became commander of the* Afrika Korps, *put the problem in a nutshell: 'A long arm is decisive–and here the British had the best of it. It was not pleasant to be exposed to the fire of their 25-pounder guns at extreme range and be unable to make an effective reply."*

Armoured Division, which had been equipped with captured Italian vehicles to replace the tanks sent to Greece. But the Italian tanks were so poor that even good British crews could not improve their performance. The 9th Australian Division (Major-General L. J. Morshead) should have reinforced this so-called armoured formation, but because of supply difficulties its foremost units had not got beyond Tobruk. The 3rd Indian Motorised Brigade completed this mediocre force.

After the capture of Benghazi, Wavell had appointed General Maitland Wilson as military governor of Cyrenaica. But the latter was recalled to Cairo and put in charge of the Greek expeditionary force immediately after taking up his command. He was succeeded by Lieutenant-General Philip Neame, V.C., a newcomer to the desert theatre, who only had a few days to accustom himself to the terrain.

The 7th Armoured Division, which had been the spearhead of XIII Corps, had been brought back to the Delta by Wavell to be completely refitted. Churchill had protested violently against this decision, and it is clear that if the division's repair shops could have been set up in Tobruk after its fall, Rommel's task would have been much harder. But it must be remembered that this first British desert offensive had been the result of successive improvisations. On December 9, 1940, O'Connor had set out on a five-day raid. By February 6, 1941, he was over 500 miles further west, at El Agheila. It was not surprising that in these totally unexpected circumstances the base facilities had not kept up with the advance of the tanks.

In any event the dispositions made by Wavell show clearly that he believed that any large-scale counter-offensive by Rommel was highly improbable. Brauchitsch and Halder also believed that Rommel's attack on Agedabia could not take place until the end of May, after the last units of 15th Panzer Division had joined his force. Again, on March 19 Hitler, decorating Rommel with the Oak Leaves to the Knight's Cross, gave him no other instructions. According to his diaries this left Rommel, eager for action, "not very happy". Benghazi, the objective given him for his spring campaign, appeared to him to be indefensible by itself. The whole of Cyrenaica must be recovered to ensure its security.

Rommel strikes

At dawn on March 24 the reconnaissance group of 5th Light Division attacked El Agheila–and the British units defending this key position pulled back without a fight. They took up new positions at Marsa Brega, between the Gulf of Sirte and salt marsh impassable to tanks, about 50 miles south-west of Agedabia.

Rommel felt that he could not stick to the letter of his orders and so leave the British with enough time to reorganise while he waited for the whole of the 15th Panzer Division to reach the front. If he attacked again without delay he had a chance of surprising the British with his small mobile forces and of dislodging them from what was an extremely strong defensive position.

He therefore attacked again on March 31. The British did put up some resistance at Marsa Brega, but, outflanked on the desert front, they were forced to give up the place to the 5th Light Division. By the evening of April 2 the German forces, followed by the "Ariete" Armoured Division and the "Brescia" Infantry Division, occupied the Agedabia region two months ahead of the schedule set by O.K.H. About 800 British prisoners were taken during this engagement. Rommel's cunning use of dummy tanks had added to the confusion of the British as they retreated; German reconnaissance aircraft saw disorganised columns streaming back towards Benghazi and Mechili.

Rommel has often been criticised for acting incorrectly; but any subordinate is entitled to pursue his own objectives if he discovers that the ones he has been given by his superiors have been based on an incorrect appreciation of the situation. And this was precisely the position when Rommel and the *Afrika Korps* reached Marsa Brega at the end of March 1941.

But in such a situation a subordinate is also supposed to inform his superiors without a moment's delay of the steps he feels himself obliged to take. Rommel failed to do so, and for days he played hide and seek with his Italian and German superiors while he breathlessly exploited his initial success.

In his book on the war in Africa General Pietro Maravigna makes this quite clear. "The covering enemy troops were surprised by the attack and withdrew. They abandoned Bir es-Suera and Marsa Brega, which Rommel's advanced forces occupied on April 1, while the main body of the 5th Light Division took up its position to the east of El Agheila.

"In Tripoli, and even more so in Rome, this news came like thunder in a clear sky. Mussolini, who was very much put out, asked Rintelen for information. Rintelen had none to give. He then asked Gariboldi to explain matters. Gariboldi replied that Rommel had evaded all authority and was acting entirely on his own initiative. Moreover, Gariboldi disclaimed all responsibility, as he had only authorised Rommel to make a surprise attack on the

△ *"The* Feldherr *of the front line"–Rommel, in an armoured car, with his men.*

The German Schwerer Panzerspähwagen (8 Rad) SdKfz 232 (Fu) armoured car

Weight: 8.3 tons.
Crew: 4.
Armament: one 20-mm cannon with 180 rounds and one 7.9-mm machine gun with 1,000 rounds.
Armour: 14-mm maximum, 8-mm minimum.
Engine: one Büssing-NAG 8-cylinder V inline, 150-hp.
Speed: 62 mph.
Range: 185 miles.
Length: 19 feet 6 inches.
Width: 7 feet 4 inches.
Height: 7 feet 9 inches (to top of turret).

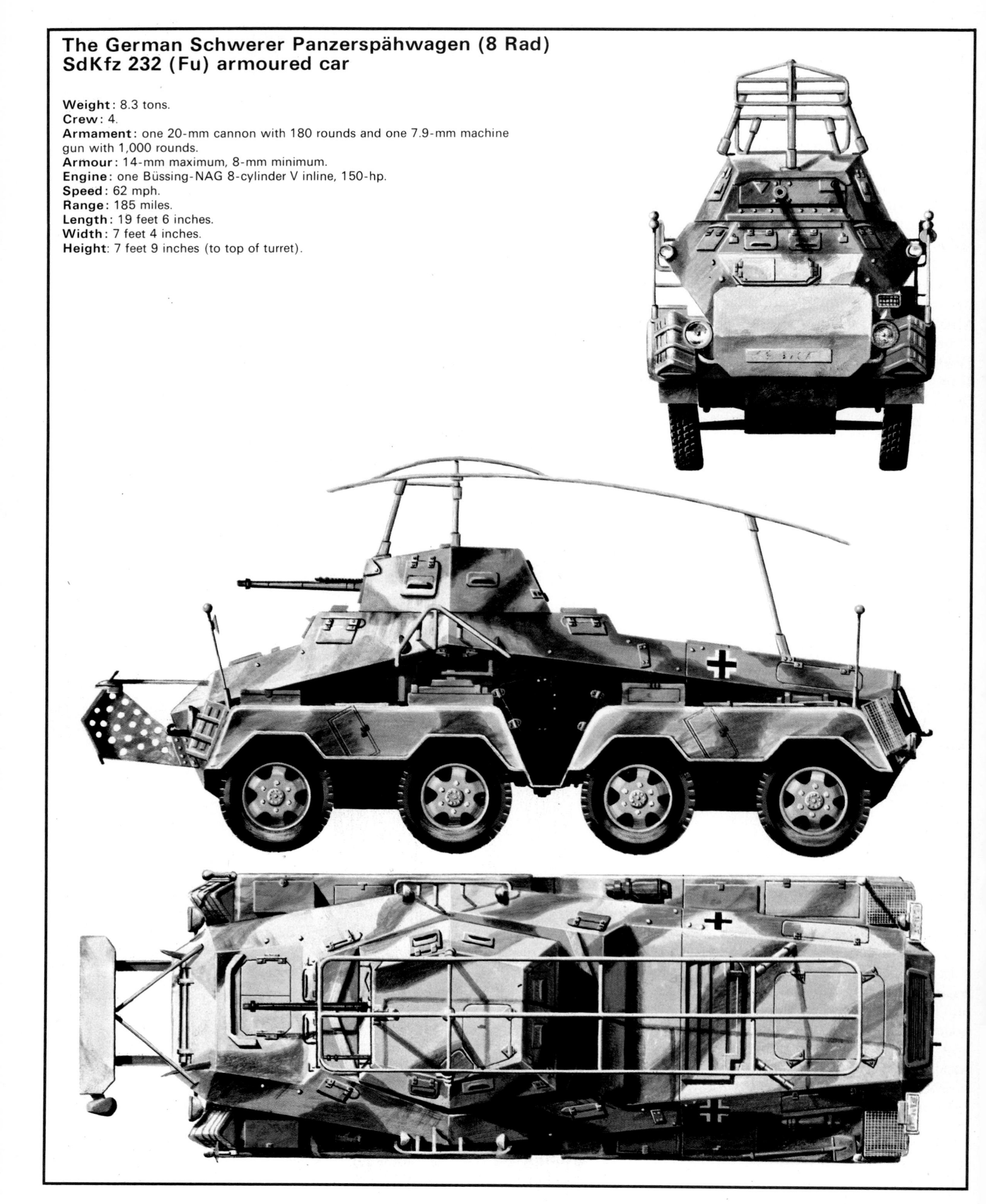

British forces west of Marsa Brega to improve our own defences; the German general, carried away by his initial success, had exceeded his authority."

Gariboldi subsequently set off after Rommel with the intention of stopping him, but he was very abruptly received by his impetuous subordinate, especially as fresh successes had provided further justification for his actions; and the German High Command in Berlin signalled its approval. In fact, on the night of April 3–4 the reconnaissance group of the 5th Light Division entered Benghazi, and its main body drove onwards towards Mechili.

In Cairo the news of Rommel's escapade caused as much bewilderment as it had to *Comando Supremo*. Neame had been ordered not to let his position be endangered if the Axis forces attacked but to make a fighting retreat; but Wavell quickly realised that Neame had been overtaken by the sudden speed of events, and that the organised retreat he had had in mind was turning into a rout.

British generals in the bag

Wavell therefore decided to call upon the services of O'Connor, but the latter had not had time to take stock of the situation before suffering an appalling stroke of ill luck. O'Connor and Neame, accompanied by General Carton de Wiart of Narvik fame, were on their way to Tmimi for a staff conference when they were captured by a German patrol near Derna.

"He was half asleep when his driver braked suddenly," writes Anthony Heckstall-Smith. "An Afrika Korps soldier shone his torch inside the car and could not suppress a cry of astonishment. Perhaps the generals could have escaped in that fraction of a second, but the soldier was rapidly joined by his comrades from the machine gun battalion commanded by Lieutenant-Colonel Ponath. O'Connor realised, too late, that his driver had veered to the north instead of steering eastward towards Tmimi.

"A few months later people in Egypt were telling the story of O'Connor's arrival at Rommel's field H.Q., when Rommel was having breakfast with his staff. O'Connor looked them up and down and asked: 'Does anyone here speak English?

"A bespectacled officer leapt to his feet, clicked his heels, bowed deeply, and said 'I do, sir.'

"'Well, get lost.'

"The story is probably apocryphal, but the soldiers in the desert army are very proud of it."

At Mechili General Gambier-Parry, commander of the 2nd Armoured Division, was also captured, along with most of his 3rd Armoured Brigade and large numbers of the 3rd Indian Motorised Brigade.

When he thrust from Agedabia to Mechili, and from Mechili to Derna, Rommel was executing O'Connor's man-

∇ *"There'll be no Dunkirk here!": Major-General Morshead* (centre), *commander of the 9th Australian Division–the defender of Tobruk.*
∇∇ *Overwhelmed by the speed of Rommel's advance–British prisoners under interrogation.*

oeuvre at Beda Fomm in reverse. But he was not so fortunate as O'Connor had been; when the advanced German units reached the Gulf of Bomba, the rearguard of the Australian brigade retreating from Benghazi had already fallen back on Tobruk and was strengthening the garrison. The Allies had escaped from the Axis net.

▽ *The miseries of a desert sandstorm – "khamseen" to the British, "ghibli" to the Germans – here experienced by two* Afrika Korps *soldiers.*

▽▽ *A German magazine illustration reflects the pride caused by the surprise capture of the British Generals O'Connor and Neame during Rommel's offensive into Cyrenaica.*

Decision to hold Tobruk

The decision to defend Tobruk at all costs was taken by Wavell on the advice of Air Chief-Marshal Longmore and Admiral Cunningham. The garrison consisted of the 9th Australian Division, reinforced by a brigade of the 7th, an armoured regiment with 45 armoured cars, and an A.A. brigade with 16 heavy and 59 light guns. All in all, there were about 36,000 men within the Tobruk perimeter.

The assault on January 21, in which Major-General Mackay had captured Tobruk, had been so rapid that the fortifications had fallen into the hands of the British almost untouched. The strongpoints, which were laid out in alternating rows, were protected by 3-foot thick concrete slabs which were proof against the heaviest guns (15-cm) the Afrika Korps had at this time. The anti-tank ditch was also intact and was still completely camouflaged with sand-covered planks.

But above all – if it is true that an army is as good as its commander – the strongest part of the Tobruk defences was Major-

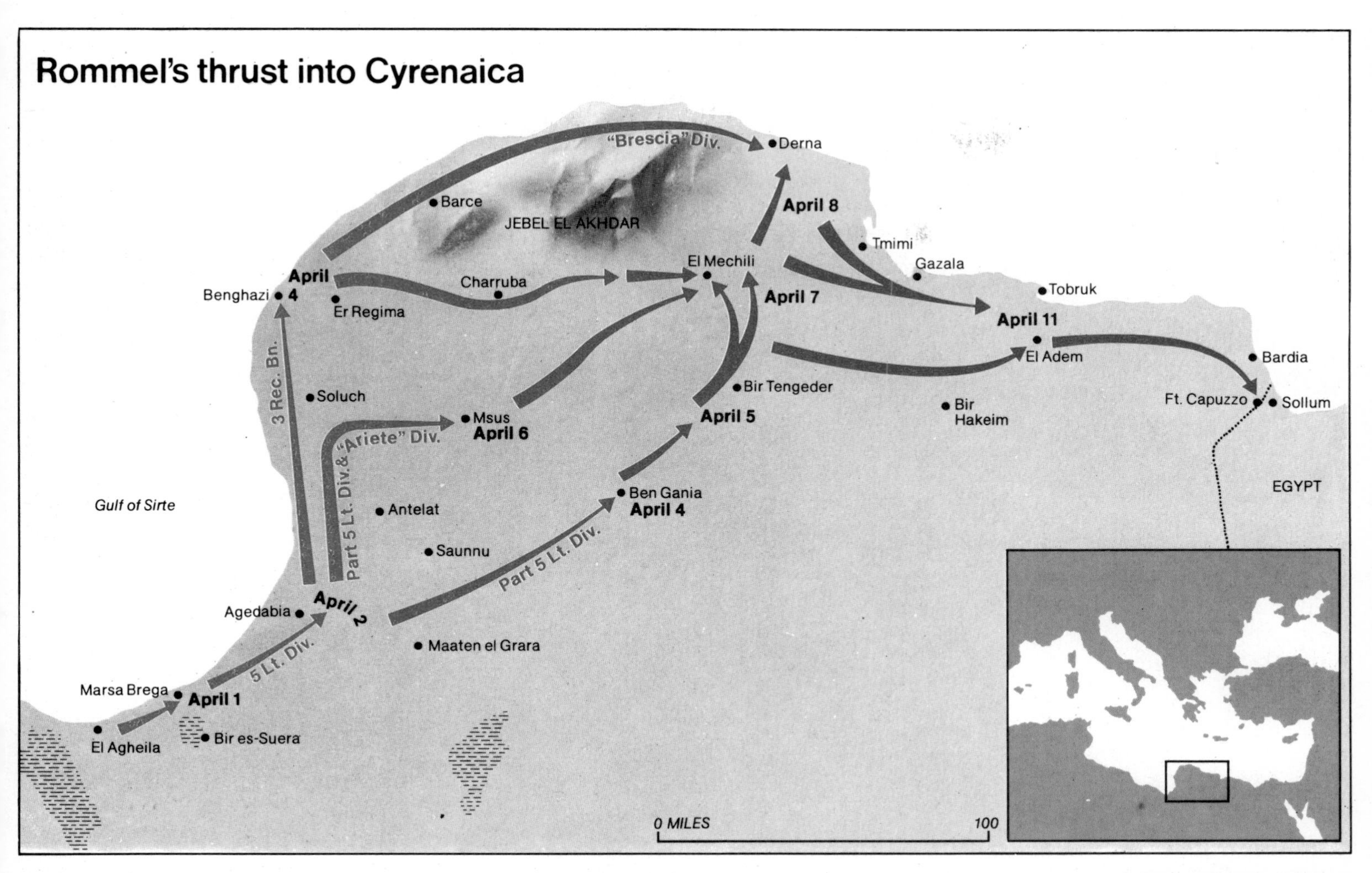

General Leslie Morshead, commander of 9th Australian Division. "There'll be no Dunkirk here!" he told his men. "If we should have to get out, we shall have to fight our way out. No surrender and no retreat."

Morshead, who had fought in World War I, had risen to the command of an infantry battalion at 20. For his bravery under fire he had been awarded the C.M.G., the D.S.O., and the *Légion d'Honneur,* and had been six times mentioned in despatches. His soldiers called him "the pitiless thing" because of his iron discipline. Another factor favouring the defenders was the comparative narrowness of the battlefield, which prevented Rommel from making his customary surprise manoeuvres.

Rommel halted at Tobruk

On April 10 Rommel tried to storm Tobruk by launching a motorised detachment under General von Prittwitz, commander of the 15th Panzer Division, to cut the coast road. But the detachment was repulsed by heavy gunfire and its commander was killed by a shell. During the night of April 13–14, a battalion of the 5th Light Division succeeded in finding a way through the minefields and crossing the anti-tank ditch. Rommel stated, however, that:

"The division's command had not mastered the art of concentrating its strength at one point, forcing a breakthrough, rolling up and securing the flanks on either side, and then penetrating like lightning, before the enemy had time to react, deep into his rear." For this reason the Panzer regiment of the 5th Light Division was overwhelmed by the concentrated fire of the Australian artillery and was unable to support the battalion which had made a "finger-probe" advance into the defences. The latter battalion was counter-attacked and virtually destroyed, leaving 250 prisoners in the hands of the Australians. Rommel was incensed by this failure, which he punished by sacking General Streich.

The Italian divisions (the "Brescia" Infantry Division, "Trento" Motorised Division, and "Ariete" Armoured Division) were even less fortunate. On the other hand, the *Afrika Korps* units covering the rear of the troops attacking

General (later Field-Marshal) Erwin Rommel was born in Heidenheim in 1891. He served with distinction in World War I. In 1938 Rommel was selected to command Hitler's escort battalion in Czechoslovakia and later in Poland, and he was appointed to the command of 7th Panzer Division in February 1940. Rommel led 7th Panzer with such success during the campaign in France that it became known as the "Ghost Division", confirming Hitler's confidence in Rommel as a daring and resourceful commander.

▲▲*Life in the desert:* Afrika Korps *armoured car crews establish themselves in new positions.*
▲ *First check for Rommel's men. His headlong charge at the strongest sector of the Tobruk defences caused heavy casualties for little gain. Here an Australian sentry guards German prisoners.*

Tobruk reoccupied the former Axis frontier positions at Sollum, Halfaya, and Capuzzo and now stood on the Egyptian frontier. But they were considerably dispersed, and although 15th Panzer Division had now joined him, Rommel realised at last that he would only be able to capture Tobruk with a well-organised attack. He lacked the resources to do this, and the regrets he expressed to O.K.H. met with a chilly reception on the part of Brauchitsch and Halder.

Halder's note of April 23 shows this clearly. "I have a feeling that things are in a mess. He [Rommel] spends his time rushing about between his widely-scattered units and sending out reconnaissance raids in which he fritters away his strength . . . no one knows exactly how his troops are deployed, nor the strength of their fighting capacity . . . He has had heavy losses as a result of piecemeal attacks. In addition his vehicles are in a bad state because of the wear and tear caused by the desert sand and many of the tank engines need replacing. Our air transport can't meet Rommel's crazy demands; we haven't enough petrol anyway, and the planes sent to North Africa wouldn't have enough fuel for the return flight."

Rommel is called to heel

But whatever Halder thought, he could only express it in his private diary, as Hitler retained full confidence in Rommel. In these circumstances, and with the approval of Brauchitsch, he merely sent Lieutenant-General Paulus, the Quartermaster-General of O.K.H., out to the North African front to obtain first-hand information.

Paulus, Halder thought, because of his

The German Panzerkampfwagen III Ausführung F

Weight: $19\frac{1}{4}$ tons.
Crew: 5.
Armament: one 5-cm KwK 39 L/42 with 99 rounds plus two 7.92-mm MG34 machine guns with 3,750 rounds.
Armour: 30-mm maximum, 16-mm minimum.
Engine: one Maybach HL 120 TRM 12-cylinder, 300-hp.
Speed: 25 mph.
Range: 105 miles.
Length: 18 feet.
Width: 9 feet 9 inches.
Height: 8 feet 1 inch.

Malta Submarines

During the first period of Luftwaffe ascendancy over Malta the main attack force based on the island consisted of the submarine flotilla, which made constant patrols against the Axis supply-lines to Tripoli. The odds were stacked heavily against the British submarines, and between April-August 1941 five of them were sunk. But between January and May of that year they accounted for 16 out of the 31 Axis ships sunk while carrying supplies and reinforcements to North Africa–a striking achievement. Simultaneous patrols were made by the destroyer flotillas based on Gibraltar and Alexandria.

◁ *Submarines of the Malta flotilla. In early 1941 the smaller, "U-class" submarines hunted in the shallow waters off the North African coast while the larger boats worked the deeper, offshore waters.*

▷▷ *More teeth for the offensive–one of the Malta submarines takes on torpedoes. To keep the Malta submarines, among other offensive weapons, supplied with fuel and torpedoes was a vital but difficult task.*

old friendship for Rommel, would "perhaps be capable of exerting some influence to head off this soldier who has gone stark mad". The special envoy of the German Army High Command carried out his delicate mission satisfactorily–but a few weeks later the entire North African theatre was transferred from O.K.H. to O.K.W. This change of the command structure eliminated any further causes of friction between the impulsive Rommel and the methodical Halder. Halder has been criticised for being unduly cautious, because his fears did not materialise. But he had no way of knowing how small were the reserve forces at the disposal of the British C.-inC. Halder was relying on the information of his Intelligence experts, who estimated that Wavell had 21 divisions, six of which were actually fighting or in the area between Tobruk, Sollum, and Halfaya.

As already mentioned, the Axis convoys which carried the 5th Light Division to North Africa had suffered insignificant losses. But the ships which carried 15th Panzer Division had a harder time.

From the time of his first meeting with General Geissler of X *Fliegerkorps*, Rommel had asked that the efforts of the German bombers should be concentrated against the port of Benghazi. Later, X *Fliegerkorps* had given very efficient air cover to the advance of the *Afrika Korps* between Agedabia and Tobruk, making up to a large extent for the heavy artillery which Rommel lacked.

The inevitable result of this was that the former pressure being applied to Malta by these air forces became considerably lighter. Admiral Cunningham was not slow to exploit this welcome and unexpected respite. Early in April he transferred a flotilla of the most modern destroyers from Alexandria to Valletta. This small force, commanded by Captain P. J. Mack, scored its first success on the night of April 14–15. It surprised an Axis convoy of five merchantmen escorted by three destroyers about 35 miles off Sfax. The convoy was silhouetted against the moon while Mack's ships were in darkness. Surprise was complete. The merchantmen were reduced to wrecks

Lieutenant-Commander Malcolm David Wanklyn *(second from left)* and fellow submarine officers. Wanklyn rapidly emerged as the most prominent British submarine ace in the Mediterranean. The *Upholder* sailed on her first patrol against the Axis supply-lines to North Africa in January 1941, and Wanklyn scored his first success by sinking the German transport *Duisburg* in the early morning of January 28. His greatest success in 1941 was the sinking of the large Italian liner *Conte Rosso* on May 25, for which he was awarded the Victoria Cross. In the desperate course of the Mediterranean War there was little respite for the submarine crews. Wanklyn and his crew were eventually lost when *Upholder* was depth-charged on April 14, 1942. He was on his twenty-third patrol and had sunk two submarines, two destroyers, and 94,900 tons of merchant shipping.

within a few minutes; 350 men, 300 vehicles, and 3,500 tons of equipment for the Afrika Korps were lost. The Italian destroyer *Baleno* was sunk, but Captain de Cristoforo of the *Tarigo*, with a leg shot off by a British shell, managed to launch three torpedoes before sinking with his ship – two of which hit and sank the British destroyer *Mohawk*.

The third Italian escort destroyer, the *Lampo*, was totally disabled and stranded on the shoals of the Kerkenna Bank, together with the German merchantman *Arta*. *Lampo* was recovered by the Italians in August and subsequently recommissioned – but in the meantime a group of French Resistance men from Tunisia had searched the derelicts by night, seized the ships' papers, and had passed on all information about the *Afrika Korps'* order of battle to Malta.

The work of the British destroyers was supplemented by that of the British submarines based on Malta and Alexandria. On February 25 the *Upright* (Lieutenant E. D. Norman) had scored a direct hit on the Italian light cruiser *Armando Diaz*, which sank in four minutes with three-quarters of her crew. In a space of four months the British submarines in the Mediterranean sank at least a dozen Axis merchantmen, tankers, and transports between Messina and Tripoli.

The submarine *Upholder*, commanded by Lieutenant-Commander Malcolm Wanklyn, a brilliant submariner, particularly distinguished herself in these actions, on which the outcome of the Desert War so much depended. On the evening of May 25 *Upholder* sank the large Italian liner *Conte Rosso* (17,879 tons), and only 1,520 out of the 2,732 sailors and soldiers aboard were saved. In recognition of this Wanklyn received the Victoria Cross.

Cunningham's troubles

Yet another consequence of the first offensive of the Afrika Korps was to create serious tension between the Admiralty and Admiral Cunningham.

Cunningham had been ordered to bom-

△ Afrika Korps *scout car in the desert. Despite the failure to take Tobruk, Rommel's reconquest of Cyrenaica meant that the initiative in the Desert War had been wrested from the British. Once again, Axis troops stood on the Egyptian frontier.*

▽ *From the* Gazzetta del Popolo *of Turin: Neptune wonders when the British Admiralty will announce the latest bump on his head in the sinkings column of* The Times.

bard Tripoli's port installations with his battle fleet, but he doubted whether the fleet's guns would be able to inflict any serious damage. He pressed for the transfer of long-range heavy bombers to Egypt, to smash the installations from the air. But this would be impossible in the immediate future. Seeking a drastic solution to the problem of Tripoli, the First Sea Lord, Sir Dudley Pound, decided that Cunningham should sacrifice the battleship *Barham* and an A.A. cruiser. Manned by skeleton crews, these would be deliberately scuttled in the entrance to Tripoli harbour.

When Cunningham received this message on April 15 he reacted with an immediate refusal. If he obeyed he would not only lose one of his three vital battleships: it was also to be feared that the *Barham* and the cruiser would be sunk by the Italians before reaching their objective. Nor was there any guarantee that the crews, however small, could be recovered, and this would mean the additional loss of about 1,000 highly-trained officers, petty officers, and ratings. But Cunningham was ready to make a compromise. Reconsidering his first objections, he stated that he was prepared to bombard Tripoli.

The Admiralty agreed, and at dawn on April 21 the battleships *Barham*, *Valiant*, and *Warspite*, with the cruiser *Gloucester*, battered Tripoli harbour for three-quarters of an hour while Swordfish from the carrier *Formidable* and aircraft from Malta assisted the warships by bombing and illuminating the port. As Cunningham had anticipated, the actual damage inflicted was not severe and had no lasting effect; but the Italians were so slow to sound the alarm that the British squadron completed its hazardous mission without suffering any harm.

Churchill's own account in *The Second World War* suggests that the responsibility for this venture rests with Sir Dudley Pound. This, however, seems unlikely. Pound would hardly have issued such a drastic order without first referring it to the Minister of Defence, Churchill. Much more likely, the initiative for the idea to scuttle the *Barham* came from Churchill. And the fact that Pound retracted his order so promptly suggests that he was being influenced by Churchill again.

CHAPTER 34
The Balkan Front

On December 29, 1940, General Ugo Cavallero, the new Chief-of-Staff of the *Comando Supremo*, was sent over by Mussolini to relieve General Ubaldo Soddu of his command and to take control of the Italian armed forces in Albania. The Duce defined Cavallero's task in a letter dated January 1: his forces were to move over to the offensive and prove, by their energy and resolve, that doubts abroad about Italian military prestige were baseless. "Germany," the letter went on, "is ready to send a mountain division into Albania and at the same time is preparing an army to attack Greece through Bulgaria in March. I am expecting, nay, I am certain, that your intervention and the bravery of your men will show that any direct support by Germany on the Albanian front will prove to be unnecessary. The Italian nation is impatiently waiting for the wind to change."

After the war General Halder drew attention to the vexing question of German reinforcements in Albania, on which Hitler and his generals never agreed:

"When the Italians got into trouble in Albania, Hitler was inclined to send help. The Army Commander-in-Chief managed to stop the plan from being put into action, as it would have been fruitless. It was a different matter when the German forces, which were actually intended for an attack on the Greeks, were ordered into Greece from Bulgaria to throw the British back into the sea. Hitler then ordered major units into northern Albania. This eccentric operation could have thrown into jeopardy any lightning success against Greece. But Hitler refused to give up his plan and his political will overrode all military objections. No harm was done, however, as the German High Command evaded executing the order, and events proved that they were right."

Δ *The Duce with his new High Command Chief-of-Staff, General Ugo Cavallero, who now had the unenviable task of trying to avert complete disaster for the Italian forces on the Albanian front.*

War in the mountains

Before Cavallero could meet the Duce's wishes he had to prevent the Greeks reaching Valona and Durazzo. At this date, to cover a front of 156 miles, he had 16 divisions, some in very bad shape and most of them poorly supplied on account of Albania's virtually non-existent communications. It is true that the opposing forces, the Greeks, who had been on the offensive since November 14, had lost a fair number of men and had only 13 divisions or their equivalent. Until such time as they could make up their strength and repair communications, General Papagos decided to abandon temporarily any idea of an all-out attack and restricted himself to limited-objective offensives. It was during one of these operations that the Greek II Corps, working as usual in the mountains, captured the important crossroads at Klisura on January 9. In a heavy snowstorm they inflicted a severe defeat on the "*Lupi di Toscana*" (Wolves of Tuscany) Division (General Ottavio Bollea), which had been force-marched to its objective. Papagos grouped his I and II Corps together under General Drakos as the Army of Epirus, but this was defeated at Telepenë in February. Not that the Greek troops lacked keenness or endurance (in his diary Cavallero says that their attacks were "frenzied"): they simply had no means of waging modern offensive warfare. This is clearly explained in the former Greek Commander-in-Chief's book on his army's operations:

"The presence among the Italian troops of a considerable number of tanks, and the fact that we had none at all and very few anti-tank guns, forced us to keep well clear of the plains, which would allow rapid movement, and to manoeuvre only in the mountains. This increased the fatigue of the men and the beasts of burden, lengthened and delayed our convoys and brought additional difficulties in command, supplies and so on. The enemy, on the other hand, thanks to the means at his disposal, was able to fall back rapidly on the plains and take up new positions without much difficulty. Taking advantage of the terrain, he was then able to hold up our advance in the mountains with a relatively small number of men. Also, the fresh troops which the Italians brought up during this phase of the war came to the front in lorries, whereas ours had to move on foot, reaching the front tired and frequently too late to be of any use. As a final point I must mention the difficulties we had in restoring the works of art which had been damaged by the enemy, and the superiority of the Italian Air Force which, after the limited daily sorties by Greek and British planes, were able to attack with impunity both our forward and our rear areas." General Cavallero's success in these defensive operations gave him enough respite to reinforce and rest his troops so as to go over to the offensive as Mussolini had ordered.

From December 29, 1940 to March 26, 1941 no fewer than ten divisions, four machine gun battalions, together with three legions and 17 battalions of Black Shirts crossed the Adriatic. When spring came the Italian land forces in Albania thus comprised: the 9th and the 11th Armies, the 9th now under General Pirzio-Biroli and the 11th still under General Geloso: six corps, with 21 infantry divisions, five mountain divisions and the "Centauro" Armoured Division. The Greeks, on the other hand, had only 13 to 14 divisions, all of them suffering from battle fatigue.

This goes to show that, though denied the Mediterranean, the Italian Navy still controlled the Adriatic. Only one difficulty faced General Cavallero: was he to give priority to bringing up reinforcements or to supplying his troops at the front, given that all the Albanian ports together, whatever might be done to increase their capacity, could only handle 4,000 tons a day? One of the few units lost during these operations was the hospital ship *Po*, torpedoed in error in Valona harbour. Countess Edda Ciano, who was serving on board as a nurse, escaped with no more than a ducking.

▽ *A Greek supply column moves through hair-raising terrain in in the Devoll river valley. These troops are on the Greek right flank, which swept forward to take Pogradec on December 4, 1940. After this the centre of gravity of the Greek offensive switched to the coastal sector, where the Greeks made gallant but unavailing efforts to take the Italian base at Valona.*

▷ *March 1941: Mussolini visits the Albanian front. By this time the situation was well in hand, and the reinforced Italian armies were on the offensive again. The Greeks held out gallantly against massive attacks, but their losses were heavy.*

Another Italian offensive

As he had re-established numerical superiority, General Cavallero now set about his offensive operations. On March 9, 1941, watched by Mussolini, the 9th Army began attacking in the sector between the river Osum (called the Apsos by the Greeks) in the north-east and the Vijosë or the Aóos in the south-west. The area is dominated by the Trebesina mountains. General Geloso put in his IV, VIII and XXV Corps (Generals Mercalli, Gambara and Carlo Rossi respectively), comprising 11 infantry divisions and the "Centauro" Armoured Division. On D-day the Greeks had three divisions and the equivalent of a fourth, all from the II Corps (General Papadopoulos). At dawn the Greek positions were heavily shelled and bombed. From their observation point, at 0830, Mussolini and Cavallero could see the infantry moving up to their objectives over territory not unlike the Carso, where so many Italians had fallen in fruitless attacks between June 1915 and August 1917.

The Trebesina offensive did not restore the Duce's prestige. Not because the Greek defenders equalled the Italian attacking force in strength, as Cavallero wrote in his diary in the evening of March 9, but because they were well organised and their morale was high. He went on: "The Greek artillery is powerfully deployed. All the elements of the defending forces are well organised in depth, using positions of strength which enable them to contain the offensive and to counter-attack immediately and vigorously."

Forty-eight hours later, not only had there not been the expected break-through, but losses were mounting, the 11th Alpini Regiment alone reporting 356 killed and wounded, including 36 officers. Should the plan be abandoned after this discouraging start? Mussolini did not think so. That very day he said to General Geloso: "The directives of the plan must be adhered to at all costs. Between now and the end of the month a military victory is vital for the prestige of the Italian Army."

And he added, with an unusual disregard for his responsibilities in the matter of Italian military unpreparedness:

General Alexander Papagos was born in 1883, and was Commander-in-Chief of the Greek forces when Italy invaded Greece on October 28, 1940. Papagos's forces not only repulsed the Italians, but also counter-attacked into Albania. His forces held the renewed Italian offensive in March 1940, but the German offensive proved too much for them in April. He was arrested and taken to Germany, where he was freed by the Americans in 1945.

▲ *Armoured help from the British: a Cruiser Mark IIA (A-10). "They were ponderous, square things," wrote Bob Crisp, a South African tank commander who went to Greece with Wavell's B.E.F.; "like mobile pre-fab houses and just about as flimsy. By far their worst failing was their complete inability to move more than a mile without breaking a track, or shedding one on a sharp turn." Crisp added: "Of the 60-odd tanks 3rd RTR had taken to Greece at the beginning of the year, not half a dozen were casualties of direct enemy action. All the others had been abandoned with broken tracks or other mechanical breakdowns. They littered the passes . . . stripped of their machine-guns, but otherwise intact. They were of no help to the enemy; no other army would have contemplated using them . . . "*

"I have always done my best to maintain the fame and the prestige of the Italian Army, but today it is vital to drive on with the offensive." They drove on, therefore, but attacks were followed by counter-attacks and General Papagos having, so to speak, thrown two divisions into the fray, the Italians were no further forward on the 15th than they had been on the 9th. When General Gambara was asked by Mussolini about the morale of his corps he replied, tactfully: "It cannot be said to be very high, but it remains firm. Losses, no territorial gains, few prisoners; this is hardly encouraging. All the same, morale is good enough not to prejudice the men's use in battle."

Mussolini and Cavallero finally drew the right conclusions from the situation and called off the attack. Mussolini returned to Rome without increasing his reputation. The three corps engaged in this unhappy affair lost 12,000 dead and wounded, or some 1,000 men per division. When it is realised that most of these losses were borne by the infantry it cannot be denied that they fought manfully.

The Greeks, on their side, however, suffered enormously and this defensive success, however honourable it might have been for their army, left them with only 14 divisions against 27.

Britain aids Greece

Meanwhile, on January 29, 1941, General Metaxas, who had forged the victories in Epirus and Albania, died suddenly in Athens and King George nominated Petros Koryzis as his successor. Events were soon to bring tragic proof that the new Greek Prime Minister could not match his predecessor in strength of character. He was, however, no less resolved to oppose with force the Germans' aggressive intentions in Rumania, as he made known in a letter to London dated February 8. This led to the departure from Plymouth on the 14th in a Sunderland flying boat bound for Cairo of Anthony Eden and Dill, the Chief of the Imperial General Staff. General Wavell raised no objections in principle to aid for Greece, in spite of the serious risks involved. Eden was thus in a position to cable the Prime Minister on February 21:

"Dill and I have exhaustively reviewed situation temporarily [*sic*] with Commanders-in-Chief. Wavell is ready to make available three divisions, a Polish brigade and best part of an armoured division, together with a number of specialized troops such as anti-tank and anti-aircraft units. Though some of these . . . have yet to be concentrated, work is already in hand and they can reach Greece as rapidly as provision of ships will allow. This programme fulfils the hopes expressed at Defence Committee that we could make available a force of three divisions and an armoured division.

"Gravest anxiety is not in respect of army but of air. There is no doubt that need to fight a German air force, instead of Italian, is creating a new problem for Longmore. My own impression is that all his squadrons are not quite up to standard of their counterpart at home . . . . . We should all have liked to approach Greeks tomorrow with a suggestion that we should join with them in holding a line to defend Salonika, but both Longmore and Cunningham are convinced that our present air resources will not allow us to do this ."

The truth is that the R.A.F. would find itself having to face not the Italian Air Force but the Luftwaffe, and that is why both Air Chief-Marshal Longmore and Admiral Cunningham doubted if the ex-

△ *Italian heavy artillery rumbles towards the front.*

▽ ◁ *Greek mountain gunners hit back at the Italians.*

peditionary force could fight on a front covering Salonika. These doubts were shared also by Sir John Dill. However, the matter was to be discussed with the Greeks at a secret conference on the following day (February 22) at the Royal Palace at Tatoi, near Athens. The results were to prove very dangerous.

The Greek viewpoint

The conference was attended by King George II, Anthony Eden, Prime Minister Koryzis, the British Ambassador in Athens, Generals Dill and Wavell, Air Chief-Marshal Longmore, and the heads of the British Military Missions in Greece. General Papagos was asked to report on the latest situation.

After giving an account of the latest Intelligence information, he put forward the solution he would advocate if Yugoslavia were to remain neutral and refuse to allow German troops to cross her territory. In this hypothesis the defence of western Thrace and eastern Macedonia would seem to be inadvisable. Troops defending the Metaxas Line, the main bulwark against Bulgaria, would therefore be given the task of slowing down the enemy advance, holding out to the last round, but the troops supporting them opposite Yugoslavia (three divisions) would fall back on a position between the lower Aliákmon river and the Vérmion and Kaïmakchalán mountains, which rise respectively to 6,725 and 8,375 feet. If all went well this operation should take about 20 days. But Papagos thought that the German forces in Rumania would need only a fortnight to get to the Bulgarian-Greek frontier from the left bank of the Danube.

Yugoslav reactions

This is where General Papagos's version disagrees with that of Eden. According to Papagos, no firm decision was taken at the end of the Tatoi conference concerning the eventual evacuation of the two provinces mentioned above. "I emphasised, however," he writes, "that after taking such a grave decision as to withdraw our troops from Thrace and eastern Macedonia and to leave this whole sector of our national territory at the mercy of the enemy without even defending it, we had to be absolutely sure about the attitude of Yugoslavia and I suggested informing the Yugoslavs about the decisions we intended to take and which would depend on their reaction."

"The British delegation," he adds, "seemed to agree and it was decided that Eden would inform H.M. Ambassador in Belgrade by urgent coded telegram. The Greek Commander-in-Chief would define his position according to the reply received. Whereupon Anthony Eden and Generals Dill and Wavell flew off to Ankara."

Eden's version is very different, though he affirms his statement on the evidence of General Wavell who died, it is true, in 1950. But, for all that, it appears that on this point, like many others, Eden's record is at variance with the events. When he got back from his fruitless journey to Ankara he sent a telegram to the Prime Minister on March 4, in which he said, among other things:

"General Papagos had on the last occasion insisted strongly that the withdrawal of all troops in Macedonia to the Aliákmon line was the only sound military solution. We expected that this withdrawal to the Aliákmon line had already begun. Instead we found that no movement had in fact commenced, Papa-

◁△ *In preparation for the new offensive: photographs of Italian Alpini in training, from the German magazine* Signal. *But when the offensive went in, the Greeks held the high ground and the Italians were compelled to attack at a disadvantage. The Alpini suffered very heavy losses.*

General Count Ugo Cavallero, born in 1880, was appointed Under-Secretary of War by Mussolini in 1925 and later became Chief-of-Staff to the Duke of Aosta in Abyssinia. He became Chief of the Italian General Staff on Badoglio's resignation in 1940, a post which he held until Mussolini's overthrow in 1943. After a spell in prison he was released, but committed suicide shortly afterwards.

△ *Italian bombing strike: Savoia-Marchetti S.M.-79's head out to the attack. Heavy bombing attacks heralded the abortive Trebesina offensive on March 9.*

▽ *Greek machine gunners get ready to hit back at the next bombing raid.*

gos alleging that it had been agreed that the decision taken at our last meeting was dependent on the receipt of an answer from Yugoslavia as to their attitude."

As we see, if this text establishes the good faith of Anthony Eden, it also shows that General Papagos's version was not thought up after the event. There was therefore a misunderstanding at Tatoi. However this may be, one thing is clear: the premature evacuation of Salonika, Yugoslavia's only possible access to the Aegean Sea, could only have a discouraging effect on Belgrade.

Bulgaria joins the Tripartite Pact

On March 1, 1941 Bulgaria joined the Tripartite Pact and the German 12th Army under Field-Marshal List crossed the Danube on pontoon bridges. In line with undertakings given on the previous January 18, this event decided the Athens Government to allow the entry into Greece of the expeditionary force organised in Cairo and put under the command of Sir Henry Maitland Wilson. But however strongly the British might have insisted, General Papagos refused to begin the anticipated withdrawal from Thrace and eastern Macedonia. It was already March 4 and everything inclined to the belief that if his three divisions on the Metaxas Line were given the order, they would now be caught in full movement.

From March 7 onwards the British Expeditionary Force began to land at the ports of Piraeus and Vólos. It was transported in 25 ships and no untoward incident occurred, as the Italian air forces based in the Dodecanese were not up to strength. Altogether 57,577 men and about 100 tanks were landed to form the 1st Armoured Brigade, the 6th Australian Division (Major-General Sir Iven Mackay) and the 2nd New Zealand Divi-

The British battleship *Warspite*

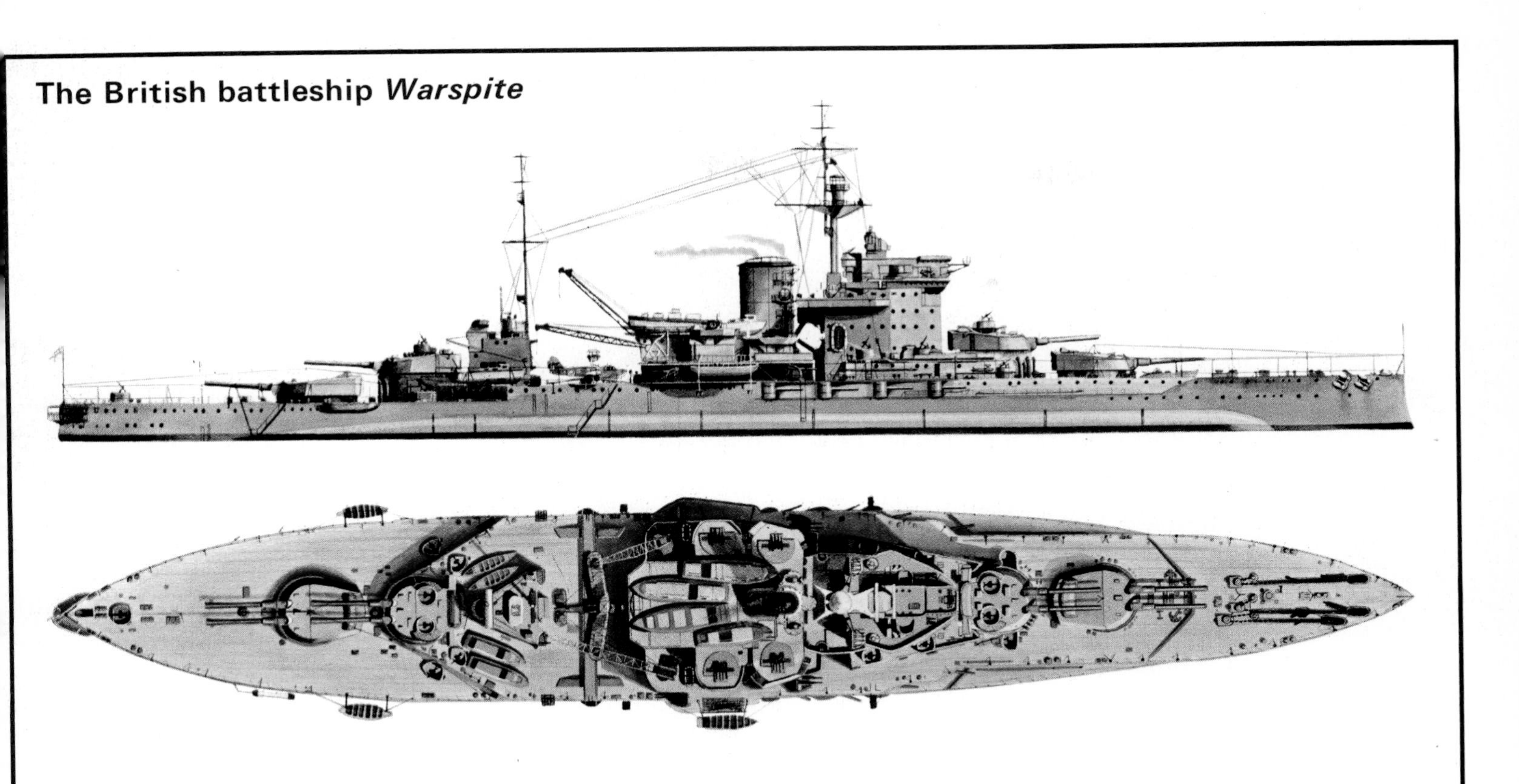

Displacement: 30,600 tons. **Armament**: eight 15-inch, eight 6-inch, eight 4-inch A.A., thirty-two 2-pdr A.A., and sixteen .5-inch guns, plus four aircraft. **Armour**: 4- to 13-inch belt, 5- to 13-inch turrets, $1\frac{1}{4}$- to 4-inch decks, and 11-inch control tower. **Speed**: 24 knots. **Length**: $639\frac{3}{4}$ feet. **Beam**: 104 feet. **Draught**: $30\frac{3}{4}$ feet. **Complement**: 1,124.

The Italian heavy cruiser *Pola*

Displacement: 11,900 tons. **Armament**: eight 8-inch, twelve 3.9-inch A.A., eight 37-mm A.A., and eight 13.2-mm guns, plus two aircraft. **Armour**: 6-inch belt, 6-inch turrets, $2\frac{3}{4}$-inch decks, and 6-inch control tower. **Speed**: 29 knots. **Length**: $599\frac{1}{2}$ feet. **Beam**: $67\frac{2}{3}$ feet. **Draught**: $19\frac{1}{2}$ feet. **Complement**: 830.

▵ *Squelching through the mud of the spring thaw, Greek supplies are brought up by mule train.*
▹ ▵ *Battle is joined off Cape Matapan: a* Bolzano-*class cruiser under Swordfish attack. This photograph, taken from the second Swordfish, shows the leading aircraft just after dropping its torpedo, the splash of which can be seen on the left of the picture.*
▹ ▿ *All sunk at Matapan.* Top to bottom: *Italian heavy cruisers* Zara *and* Pola, *with the* Oriani-*class destroyer* Giosue Carducci.

sion, the latter under Major-General Bernard Freyberg, V.C., a hero of the Dardanelles and the Somme.

At the end of the month Maitland Wilson's troops were in position behind the Aliákmon and the Vérmion mountains. On the other hand, after negotiations which, in a telegram dated March 4, Eden describes somewhat testily as "bargaining more reminiscent of oriental bazaars", the Greek High Command put under the B.E.F. three divisions (the 12th, the 20th, and the 19th Motorised) with seven battalions withdrawn from the Turkish border after reassurances from Ankara. The British expected more of their allies, but it should be noted on the other hand, that the 7th Australian Division (Major-General J. D. Lavarack) and the 1st Polish Brigade (General Kopanski), which should have been sent to Greece, never left the Middle East.

Joint plans

On February 14 at Merano, Grand-Admiral Raeder had recommended Admiral Riccardi to be more active. The transportation of the expeditionary force to Greece gave *Supermarina* the chance of intervening in the Eastern Mediterranean. The German and Italian G.H.Q.'s encouraged these impulses towards an offensive all the more keenly because on March 16 the X *Fliegerkorps* announced, wrongly as it turned out, that its planes had torpedoed two of the three battleships of the Mediterranean Fleet and put them out of action.

The plan was to sweep the Aegean and Mediterranean on D-day with two detachments as far as the island of Gávdhos, 31 miles south of Crete. The task force was put under the command of Rear-Admiral Angelo Iachino and consisted of the battleship *Vittorio Veneto*, six heavy and two light cruisers, and 13 destroyers. The operation also required considerable air support, both for reconnaissance and for defence against British bombers and torpedo-carrying aircraft.

Agreement was reached on joint air support with both the Italian Air Force and the Luftwaffe's X *Fliegerkorps*, but there was no time to test the arranged procedures in exercises. It is true that there were German and Italian liaison officers on board the *Vittorio Veneto*, but on the whole Admiral Iachino was sceptical of the results to be expected from this improvised collaboration, particularly concerning fighter support.

The Battle of Matapan

In the afternoon of March 27 a Sunderland flying boat spotted the squadron, which was then steaming through the Ionian Sea. The British had thus been alerted, as decoded messages subsequently confirmed, and it was now unlikely that any of their convoys could be intercepted. Yet the only offensive orders countermanded by *Supermarina* were those concerning the area north of Crete. That same evening Cunningham slipped out of Alexandria with three battleships and the aircraft-carrier *Formidable*, which had 37 aircraft on board. He had arranged a rendezvous south-east of Gávdhos with Vice-Admiral H. D. Pridham-Wippell's squadron of four cruisers from Piraeus.

First contact, at about 0800 hours, was between Admiral Sansonetti's three heavy cruisers and Pridham-Wippell's light cruisers. Though the British ships mounted only 6-inch guns against the Italian vessels' 8-inch, their evasive

action, contrary to the Royal Navy's tradition of aggressiveness, led Iachino to think that they might be acting as bait for a large ship as yet out of sight. He therefore recalled Sansonetti. Pridham-Wippell then gave chase, only to find himself being fired on by the *Vittorio Veneto*'s 15-inch guns. The Italians loosed off 94 rounds but failed to score a hit. Then at about mid-day torpedo-carrying aircraft from the *Formidable* launched a first attack, but without success. Admiral Iachino thereupon headed back to base.

At 1510 hours, the Fleet Air Arm launched its second attack. At the cost of his life, Lieutenant-Commander J. Dalyell-Stead dropped his torpedo at very short range and severely damaged the *Vittorio Veneto*, causing her to ship 4,000 tons of water and putting her two port engines out of action. Thanks to the efforts of her crew the damaged battleship got under way again at a speed of first 17 then 19 knots.

By this time Cunningham, with the main body of his fleet, was about 87 miles away. The *Formidable*'s planes kept him fully informed of the Italian movements, whereas Iachino was in complete ignorance of Cunningham's, and was no better informed than he had been defended by the exiguous Axis air support. In despair, and relying on a radio bearing from *Supermarina*, Iachino admitted that he was being chased by an aircraft-carrier and a cruiser some 170 miles away.

As daylight faded he gathered about the damaged flagship his 1st and 3rd Cruiser Squadrons and the destroyers in case another attack was made by British aircraft. These had, in fact, been ordered to delay the *Vittorio Veneto* so that the British battleships could finish her off. Iachino's defensive tactics, including the use of smoke screens, prevented this, but towards 1925 hours the heavy cruiser *Pola* was torpedoed. Iachino ordered Admiral Cattaneo to stay with the *Pola*, taking her in tow if possible and scuttling her if this proved impracticable. The decision was later criticised, but was justified in the light of Iachino's estimate of the British position. However this may be, the luckless cruiser then came up on the *Ajax*'s radar screen. Pridham-Wippell took her for the *Vittorio Veneto* and signalled to Cunningham, who was closing with the *Warspite*, *Valiant*, and *Barham*. At about 2200 hours *Valiant*'s radar picked up Cattaneo's cruisers sailing blindly forward into the darkness. Some 30 minutes later the British squadron's 24 15-inch guns blasted them out of the water at point-blank range. The

△ *Italian* Zara*-class heavy cruiser. Three of these splendid 8-inch gun cruisers–*Zara, Pola, *and* Fiume*–were sunk at Matapan. The fourth* (Gorizia) *was not involved in the battle.*

▷ *The Battle of Matapan. Only the escape of the damaged battleship* Vittorio Veneto *marred Cunningham's triumph, which prevented the likelihood of any Italian surface interference with the shipping of troops and supplies to Greece.*

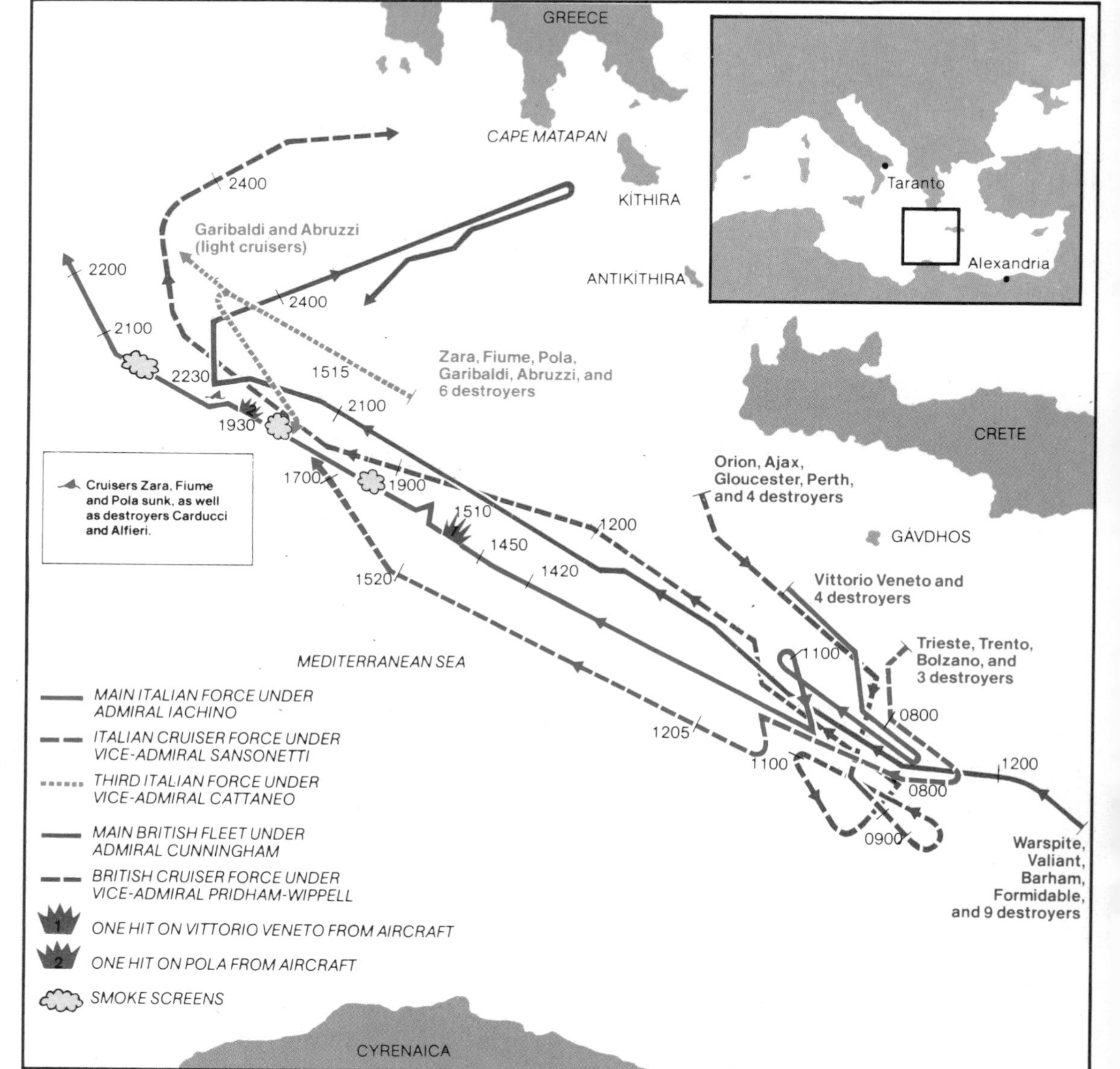

▽ *The boast made good at Matapan.*

Fiume went down at 2315 hours, the *Zara*, which was sinking more slowly, was scuttled by her commander and the destroyers *Alfieri* and *Carducci* met a similar fate. Finally a British destroyer sank *Pola* after picking up her survivors.

That night and the morning after the battle, which took place 112 miles southwest of Cape Matapan, the British, with the aid of some Greek torpedo boats, picked up just over a thousand survivors. The rescue operations were hampered by a Luftwaffe attack, but Cunningham generously signalled Rome, giving the area where further survivors might still be found. The hospital ship *Gradisca* subsequently picked up another 160. Altogether 2,400 Italian seamen were lost, including Admiral Cattaneo and the commanders of the cruisers *Zara* and *Fiume*, Captains Giorgis and Corsi respectively. The only British loss was that of the heroic Dalyell-Stead.

Although Admiral Cunningham was not altogether satisfied with the outcome of the battle, since the *Vittorio Veneto* had got away and reached Taranto, Cape Matapan was a heavy defeat for the Italian Navy, which had lost at one blow three of its 12,000-ton cruisers, a loss which could not be made good overnight. This was what Mussolini had in mind when he received Admiral Iachino at the Palazzo Venezia.

"The operation promised well and might have been successful had it not been for the total lack of co-operation from the air arm. During the whole time you never had a single Italian or German plane over you. All the aircraft you saw were the enemy's. They chased you, attacked you, overpowered you. Your ships were like blind invalids being set upon by several armed killers."

Naval operations were impossible in British-controlled waters without proper reconnaissance and fighter support. Mussolini concluded, with what Iachino describes as the true journalist's capacity for summing things up: "And as fighter aircraft have a limited range, the ships must take their escorts with them. In a word, all naval forces must always be accompanied by at least one aircraft-carrier."

And so the Duce was going back on the point of view he had expressed in 1930, but late in view of a defeat which was to weigh heavily on Italian strategy. To alleviate the consequences it was decided to convert two liners, *Roma* and *Augustus*, into aircraft-carriers and rename them *Aquila* and *Sparviero*. Until they came into service the fleet was forbidden to sail outside land-based fighter range.

The exploit of Lieutenant Faggioni and his five men in the battle of Cape Matapan deserves not to be forgotten. During the night of March 25–26 they managed to get into Suda Bay, on the north coast of Crete, in motor boats loaded with explosives. There they crippled the cruiser *York* and the oil-tanker *Pericles*.

▽ *Italy's belated attempt to match the superiority given to the Mediterranean Fleet by the activity of the Fleet Air Arm: the aircraft-carrier* Aquila. *The decision to build a carrier for the Italian Navy was finally taken after Matapan. The passenger liner SS* Roma *was taken over for complete conversion. She was given the 4-shaft turbine engines from the unfinished light cruisers* Cornelio Silla *and* Paolo Emilio, *which were intended to enable her to make 30 knots. The hull was armoured with a bulge of reinforced concrete 600-mm thick. Twin catapults were installed for launching her air group, which would have consisted of a maximum of 51 Reggiane 2001 fighters.* Aquila *was virtually ready for sea trials when Italy signed the armistice with the Allies in 1943. She was captured by the Germans, who scuttled her in 1945.*

CHAPTER 35
Yugoslavia & Greece

The entry of German troops into Bulgaria, the import of which escaped no one in Europe, put Yugoslavia in a difficult position. In face of the claims on her territory by Italy, Hungary, and Bulgaria, was she to go on defying the Third Reich by refusing to join the Tripartite Pact? And had not Hitler said that he did not intend to pass through Yugoslav territory to invade Greece?

It has been said that this guarantee was a trap, but it seems unlikely. It must be remembered that when List and his H.Q. were told that they could in future use Yugoslav territory to turn the Metaxas Line they greeted the news with feelings of great relief. This permission must clearly have been denied to them previously, doubtless because Hitler looked upon the Yugoslav Army as the rightful heirs of the brave Serbian Army of 1914–1918.

By joining the Tripartite Pact on March 25, the Regent, Prince Paul, and the Prime Minister, Dragisa Cvetković, did not choose to tread the hero's path, but before condemning them it must be realised that a discreet sounding of opinion in Athens had revealed to them that very little was to be expected of the British. On the other hand they were doubtless better informed of the ruinous situation within Yugoslavia than the military faction who overthrew them two days later.

Military coup d'état in Belgrade

Was the British Ambassador an accessory to the military plot in Belgrade on March 27, when the young King Peter's majority was proclaimed and General Simović assumed power? It was said so at the time and we know now that when he heard that the Regent had decided to sign the Tripartite Pact, Anthony Eden telegraphed Sir Ronald Campbell on March 24:

"You are authorized now to proceed at your discretion by any means at your disposal to move leaders and public opinion to understanding of realities and to action to meet the situation.

"You have my full authority for any measures that you may think it right to take to further change of Government or régime, even by *coup d'état*."

But did King George VI's representative in Belgrade have time to carry out these new instructions? It would appear not. However this may be, the new masters in Yugoslavia showed a marked lack of determination in both the diplomatic and the military field, and continued to hope that the crisis would be resolved without recourse to war. They thus took care not

◁ April 1941: Operation "Marita" begins. German forces move into Greece to eliminate the troublespot created by Mussolini's ill-starred invasion in October 1940.

▽ Brief relaxation for some Panzer crewmen–a game of cards and accordion music.

to provoke the Third Reich by, for instance, denouncing the Tripartite Pact or proclaiming general mobilisation. This gave Hitler time to overtake them and seize the initiative.

Hitler decides to attack Yugoslavia

Before the day of March 27 was over Hitler had signed the 13 copies of his Directive No. 25. This declared in its first paragraph: "The military revolt in Yugoslavia has changed the political position in the Balkans. Yugoslavia, even if it makes initial professions of loyalty, must be regarded as an enemy and beaten down as soon as possible." Having defined the principle he went on to the means of execution. Two strategic groups, one from the Fiume-Graz front and the other from the Sofia area, would converge on Belgrade and wipe out the Yugoslav Army. A third group would attack Serbian Macedonia to secure a base for the Italo-German attack on Greece. An attempt would be made to bring in Hungary and Bulgaria by guaranteeing that their territorial claims would be met. Assurances of national self-determination to the Croats would intensify political tension in Yugoslavia.

On the same day Belgrade had 900,000 men under arms and a mobilisation decree would have brought in another 500,000.

But to carry out the Führer's orders within the time required to achieve surprise, a necessary condition for a quick success, the German High Command had to draw heavily on its preparations for "Barbarossa", thus delaying the attack on the Soviet Union from mid-May to late June. In fact Operation "Marita", revised and extended in next to no time by admirable staff work, involved two armies and *Panzergruppe* Kleist: ten corps, four of which were armoured – 32 divisions, including ten armoured and four motorised or their equivalent in all. Events moved so rapidly, however, that eight of these divisions could not get to the front in time.

As was to be expected, Mussolini welcomed Hitler's initiative, which would allow him to realise his long-cherished dream of crushing Yugoslavia. To this effect 2nd Army was concentrated in Venezia Giulia under the command of General Ambrosio, with four corps (14 divisions, including the "Pasubio" and "Torino" Motorised Divisions and the "Littorio" Armoured Division). Another division was to attack from Zara, while 11th Army in Albania would attempt to link up with the Germans in Serbian Macedonia.

On the promise that Hungarian claims on Yugoslavia would be met, Admiral Horthy felt obliged to join in the attack, in spite of the non-aggression pact he had signed a few weeks previously with Prince-Regent Paul. His Foreign Minister, Count Teleki, committed suicide over this breach of promise.

▽ "Marita"–the German invasion of Greece–was matched by "Punishment", the crushing of Yugoslavia. Here a Yugoslav civilian helps a German Army officer get his bearings.

Yugoslavia crushed

The defeat of Yugoslavia and her armed forces took 12 days. On April 6 units of *Luftflotte* IV under Colonel-General Alexander Löhr savagely bombed Belgrade while *Panzergruppe* Kleist began the assault. The XIV Motorised Corps (General von Wietersheim) advanced along a line Sofia – Niš, immediately took the Tsaribrod col and covered 312 miles in

Balkan Campaign
GRECO-ITALIAN FRONT ON APRIL 6, 1940
ITALIAN OPERATIONS
GERMAN ADVANCES
BOUNDARY BETWEEN 2ND AND 12TH ARMIES
METAXAS LINE
BRITISH MOVEMENTS
AIRBORNE OPERATIONS
Vienna
AUSTRIA
Budapest
HUNGARY
Danube
Klagenfurt
2nd Army
Italian 2nd Army
Drava
XLVI Pz. Corps
XLI Pz.Corps (part of Pz.Gruppe Kleist)
Ljubljana
Zagreb
Barcs
Timişoara
Trieste
Venice
Karlovac
Fiume
Novi Sad
Sava
Ruma
Pula
Banja Luka
Belgrade
Zara
Sarajevo
Ancona
Spálato (Split)
Drina
Morava
Niş
12th Army
Pz.Gruppe Kleist (XIV Mot.& XI Corps)
Sofia
YUGOSLAVIA
XL Mot. Corps.
Kyustendil
XVIII Mountain Corps.
XXX Corps.
Kotor
Pescara
Adriatic Sea
Rome
Scutari
Skopje
Kočani
Delčevo
Veles
Rupel
Tirana
ALBANIA
ITALY
Vardar
Bitola
Sérrai
Dojran
Kilkis
Lake Ohrida
Devolli
Bari
Naples
Flórina
Vérmion
Salonika
Kaïmakchalán
Brindisi
Vijose
Aliakmon
Valona
Taranto
Tepelenë
Ersekë
Grevená
Kozáni
Olympus
Métsovon
Yanina
Trikkala
Lárisa
Vólos
XL Mot. Corps.
Thermopylai
GREECE
Ionian Sea
Náupaktos
Thebes
Megara
Athens
Rafina
Piraeus
Pto Rafti
Corinth
Náuplion
Kalamata
Monemvasía
Messina
Palermo
Reggio di Calabria
Catania
Comiso
Syracuse
MALTA
Máleme
Rethimnon
Heraklion
Khóra Sfakion
CRETE
Hierapetra
Iasi (Jassy)
Chisinau
Galati
Izmail
Sibiu
Braşov
Braila
RUMANIA
Bucharest
Constanța
Craiova
Danube
Varna
BULGARIA
Burgas
Istanbul
Sea of Marmara
Thasos
Lesbos
TURKEY
Aegean Sea
Chios
Samos
Rhodes
Tripoli
Derna
El Marj (Barce)
Benghazi
Tobruk

seven days along the Morava valley. On April 13, in the ruins of the unhappy capital, it met the XLI Panzer Corps (General Reinhardt) which had advanced from the Timişoara area.

Except for its 5th Panzer Division, *Panzergruppe* Kleist then came under 2nd Army, which had concentrated in Carinthia and southern Hungary under the command of Colonel-General von Weichs. As soon as it was engaged in battle its XLVI Panzer Corps (General von Vietinghoff) launched a surprise attack on a bridge over the Drava at Barcs, captured it and opened the way for the headlong rush of this latest Blitzkrieg. Without stopping at Zagreb, the 14th Panzer Division made its first contact with the Italian 2nd Army at Karlovac, then sped on through Banja Luka towards Sarajevo, which it occupied on April 15. Between the Sava and the Drava the 8th Panzer and the 16th Motorised Divisions drove on just as easily through Novi Sad and Ruma, then up the Drina valley to join forces with the 14th Panzer Division. Meanwhile *Panzergruppe* Kleist had moved from Belgrade to Kruševac to block the escape route of any Yugoslav remnants trying to get from Bosnia into Macedonia.

The way the campaign developed shows that Peter II's armies not only had obsolete weapons but had been caught in indefensible positions. It must also be stated that Mussolini and Ciano's undermining of morale in Croatia over the years had at last borne its rotten fruit. There is proof of this in this note from Colonel-General Halder, who was in Wiener-Neustadt with Brauchitsch:

"April 11, Good Friday . . . Information gathered during the course of the day gives the impression that in the north of Yugoslavia the front is breaking up with increasing rapidity. Units are laying down their arms or taking the road to captivity, according to our airmen. One cycle company captures a whole brigade with its staff. An enemy divisional commander radios his superior officer that his men are throwing down their arms and going home."

One more indication, among others, of this lack of morale: the Yugoslav fleet never attempted to get into British-controlled waters, and even let most of its ships fall into Axis hands undamaged. In particular there were three destroyers which the Italian Captain Bragadin describes as "very modern" and of whose

▽ *The remorseless efficiency of the German Army machine. Wehrmacht troops pour through a village, passing transport abandoned by the retreating Yugoslav Army.*

capture he boasts as a proud accession to the Italian Navy. The only vessel of this class denied to the Axis was the *Zagreb*, which her commander scuttled.

Under these conditions it is not surprising that on April 17, 1941 the Yugoslav Foreign Minister, Aleksander Cincar-Marković, and General Janković, the Deputy Chief-of-Staff, went to Belgrade to sign the instrument of surrender drawn up by Colonel-General von Weichs and the Italian Military Attaché. King Peter II boarded a Sunderland flying boat at Kotor and left for Egypt.

Colonel Mihailović continues the struggle

As a consequence of the surrender of April 17, 6,028 Yugoslav officers and 337,684 N.C.O.s and men became prisoners-of-war. Almost 300,000 men of the conquered army, mainly Serbs, succeeded, however, in escaping captivity. Many of them continued to fight under Colonel Draža Mihailović, who had played an important part in the *Putsch* on

△ *With the experience of three victorious campaigns behind them, German anti-aircraft crewmen take up position to cover one of their main supply roads.*
◁ *Communications duties. A German motorcyclist roars along a dusty track on a mission to Thebes.*

March 27. On the other side of the scales, the German High Command figures, confirmed after the end of the war, gave 151 killed, 15 missing, and 392 wounded. This is further proof of the causes of the Yugoslav collapse mentioned above.

Though they were no more able to escape defeat than the Yugoslavs, the Greeks nevertheless cut a much better figure, although uncertainties as to the eventual direction of Belgrade's policies continued to affect the decisions of the

Greek High Command. On March 25, hearing that Cvetković had signed the Tripartite Pact, General Papagos ordered the Metaxas Line and Salonika to be abandoned. He countermanded this order on the 27th, when he learnt of the upsurge of patriotism which had carried Simović to power. During the night of April 4–5, accompanied by Anothony Eden and Sir John Dill, he met General Janković on the Greco-Yugoslav border. According to his account, the latter guaranteed that the Strumica area would be solidly defended; with this door to invasion securely locked and bolted, a concentric attack, in which both countries would share, would be mounted against Albania. His Yugoslav colleague's intention of defending an over-long frontier by 1920-type methods seemed to Papagos to be strategic heresy.

But advisers are not the ones who pay. Papagos could not persuade Janković to abandon two-thirds of his national territory in the interests of common defence. Yet reports were piling up in his headquarters to the effect that a German attack was imminent. Therefore on April 6, at 0100 hours, he ordered demolitions to be carried out between the Bulgarian frontier and the forward Greek defence positions.

The defence of northern Greece

Zero hour came at 0515. According to the plan, western Thrace, between the Greek frontier and the Néstos, was to be abandoned to its fate. On the other hand, the right bank of the Néstos was to be defended to the last man, as also was the Metaxas Line, so as to link up with the Yugoslavs in the area of Strumica. The force to be used was the Army of Macedonia (General Bakopoulos) comprising the "Evros" and the "Néstos" Divisions, the 7th Division, General Dedes's group (the 14th and the 18th Divisions), and the Kroúsia group, which was in touch with the Yugoslav forces. Resistance would be based on the Metaxas Line fortifications, which were modern, well-planned, and manned by an élite garrison.

Opposite these Greek forces, Field-Marshal List crossed the Greco-Bulgarian frontier with five divisions from the XXX Corps (General Ott) in the east and the XVIII Mountain Corps (General Böhme) in the west. The attack was supported from the air by Stukas of VIII *Fliegerkorps*. But, and this was unique in Europe, the fortifications of the Metaxas Line included A.A. turrets with 37-mm guns, which minimised the effect of the dive-bombers.

Wherever the Greeks had not previously been ordered to retreat, they held out desperately and often with success. When it reached the Néstos, the German XXX Corps was driven back as it tried to cross. In the Nevrokop basin the 72nd Division (Lieutenant-General Mattenklott) lost 700 killed and wounded in three days as it tried to break out towards Sérrai and Salonika; twice its pioneers got inside the outer defences at Perithórion and twice they were driven back. In the Rupel pass the reinforced regiment which was attacking lost a quarter of its men in fire from the fortifications and was unable to reach any of its objectives. The 5th and 6th Mountain Divisions under Generals Ringel and Schörner were more fortunate. The forts at Istibey and Kelkayia were too

◁ Stuka crew prepares for take-off.
◁◁▽ Bf 109 fighter pilot is helped into his flying kit by a ground crewman.
◁▽ The eyes of the German Army–a Henschel Hs 126 observation aircraft.
▽ Defeat. Beaten Yugoslav soldiers, carrying improvised white flags, struggle across a river to surrender.

△ *The watch on the coast–German machine gunners on the Aegean Sea.*
▷ *Advanced infantry mark their position for the benefit of the Luftwaffe by spreading a German flag across the rocks.*

close to the Bulgarian frontier and were put partially out of action by shots fired through their embrasures by 5-cm anti-tank guns and 2-cm and 8·8-cm A.A. guns, which had been lined up before D-day but had not been attacked by the Greeks. Nevertheless, the Greeks defended the approaches, then the main positions of their forts until they had been all but asphyxiated by the carbon dioxide released by numerous underground explosions. At Kelkayia, at mid-day on April 7, Captain Zakynthos surrendered 154 men, unwounded, but most of them poisoned, out of 264; at Istibey, before ordering them to lay down their arms at 1600 hours, Major Pitoulakis had lost 143 men killed and wounded out of a garrison of 457. For its part the 5th Mountain Division had lost the equivalent of a battalion. In the Kroúsia sector, which was less well organised, the 6th Mountain Division made good progress.

But the fate of the Greek forces fighting in Macedonia as well as the future of the Greek and Balkan campaign were being decided here and now and irrevocably by the successes of the 2nd Panzer Division (Lieutenant-General Vieil) at Strumica and of the XL Motorised Corps (General Stumme) on the Kyustendil col. Operating

on the right wing of the XVIII Mountain Corps inside Yugoslavia, the 2nd Panzer Division had reached Strumica, over 19 miles from its point of departure, before nightfall, knocking out the "Bregalnica" Division on its way. At dawn on the 8th, having occupied the right bank of Lake Dojran, it crossed the Greek frontier. The 19th Motorised Infantry Division tried to block its path at Kilkís, but according to the history of this campaign published by G.H.Q. Athens, the division's equipment was "tragi-comical" and so, in the evening of the same day, after a dash of some 56 miles, Vieil occupied Salonika. With his communications cut, General Bakopoulos was ordered to surrender and he commanded his 70,000 men to lay down their arms at 1400 hours on April 9.

The defeat of Yugoslavia seals the fate of Greece

It took the XL Motorised Corps 48 hours to get its 9th Panzer Division from Kyustendil to Skopje and its 73rd Division to Kočani and Veles, demolishing on the way the "Morava" and "Ibar" Divisions. So complete was the surprise that seven Yugoslav generals fell into the hands of the Germans along with 20,000 men and at least 100 guns. Stumme then changed the *Leibstandarte Adolf Hitler*'s axis of advance from west to south and on April 9 it seized the important crossroads at Bitola or Monastir. Forty-eight hours later the "Chumadia" and "Vardar"

▽ The eternal watch of the Luftwaffe–Ju 88 bombers.
▽▽ German mountain troops push into the highlands of Greece to extend their hold over the country.

Divisions had been put out of action, while the XL Motorised Corps made its first contact with the Italian 9th Army in the area of Ohrid. The collapse of the Yugoslav 3rd Army brought the right wing of the German 12th Army up against the rear positions along the line Aliákmon – Vérmion – Kaïmakchalán, occupied by Maitland Wilson and his Anglo-Greek force. Air Vice-Marshal D'Albiac's Gloster Gladiators, which had swept Mussolini's Fiat C.R. 42's out of the sky, were now unfortunately being hounded by Messerschmitt 109's from *Luftflotte* IV as these opened the way for the Stukas. On the ground, the British 1st Armoured Brigade had 100 tanks, most of them obsolete, against Field-Marshal List's possible 500 or even 600, when the 5th Panzer Division rejoined the XL Motorised Corps. All the evidence pointed to the necessity of retreat in both Macedonia and Albania. Perhaps General Papagos decided on it too late. What is certain is that the XVIII Mountain Corps forced the Aliákmon in spite of resistance from the 2nd New Zealand Division, skirted Mount Olympus and occupied Lárisa on April 18, while the XL Mountain Corps, adding to the outflanking movement, pushed forward along the line Flórina – Kozáni – Tríkkala. Through lack of mobile reserves and insufficient co-ordination of movement between the two Allies, a breach opened up between the left of the B.E.F. and the right of the Greek armies slowly withdrawing from Albania.

▽ Greek wounded in captivity. Despite their rapid defeat after months of victorious resistance against the Italians, the spirit of the Greeks – military and civilian – was unbroken. One British Intelligence officer, preparing to sail from Athens to Crete, found a scrawled note in his car which read: "Great Britain forever victorious! We are all with you, the whole nation, and are waiting and looking forward to your coming back and setting us free."

Sixteen divisions surrender

The *Leibstandarte Adolf Hitler* reached and swept through Grevená, took the Métzovon col and, on April 21, captured Yanina in the rear of the Greeks. Against orders from Athens and over the head of his superior, General Drakos, the commander of the Army of Macedonia, General Tzolakoglou entered into negotiations with the Germans, an action in which he was supported by his corps commanders and the Bishop of Yanina.

The instrument of capitulation, which led to the surrender of 16 Greek divisions, was signed at Lárisa by a representative of the Greek Parliament and Field-Marshal List. Mussolini's anger at this rattled the window panes of the Palazzo Venezia. Hitler then ordered the commander of the 12th Army to organise a new signing ceremony to which the representatives of his friend Mussolini were to be invited. The derisory event took place at Salonika on April 24, 1941, and thus it was that the Fascist dictator came to triumph over the Greeks whom he had not conquered. Some 140,000 Greeks had capitulated under these terms.

B.E.F. to be evacuated

Meanwhile, on April 19, a conference between the Allies had been held in Athens to take stock of the situation. King George II and Generals Papagos, Wavell, and Maitland Wilson were present and by common consent they decided that the British Expeditionary Force would evacuate the mainland of Greece.

The subsequent fighting at Thermopylai, then before Thebes, was aimed solely at covering this operation, the

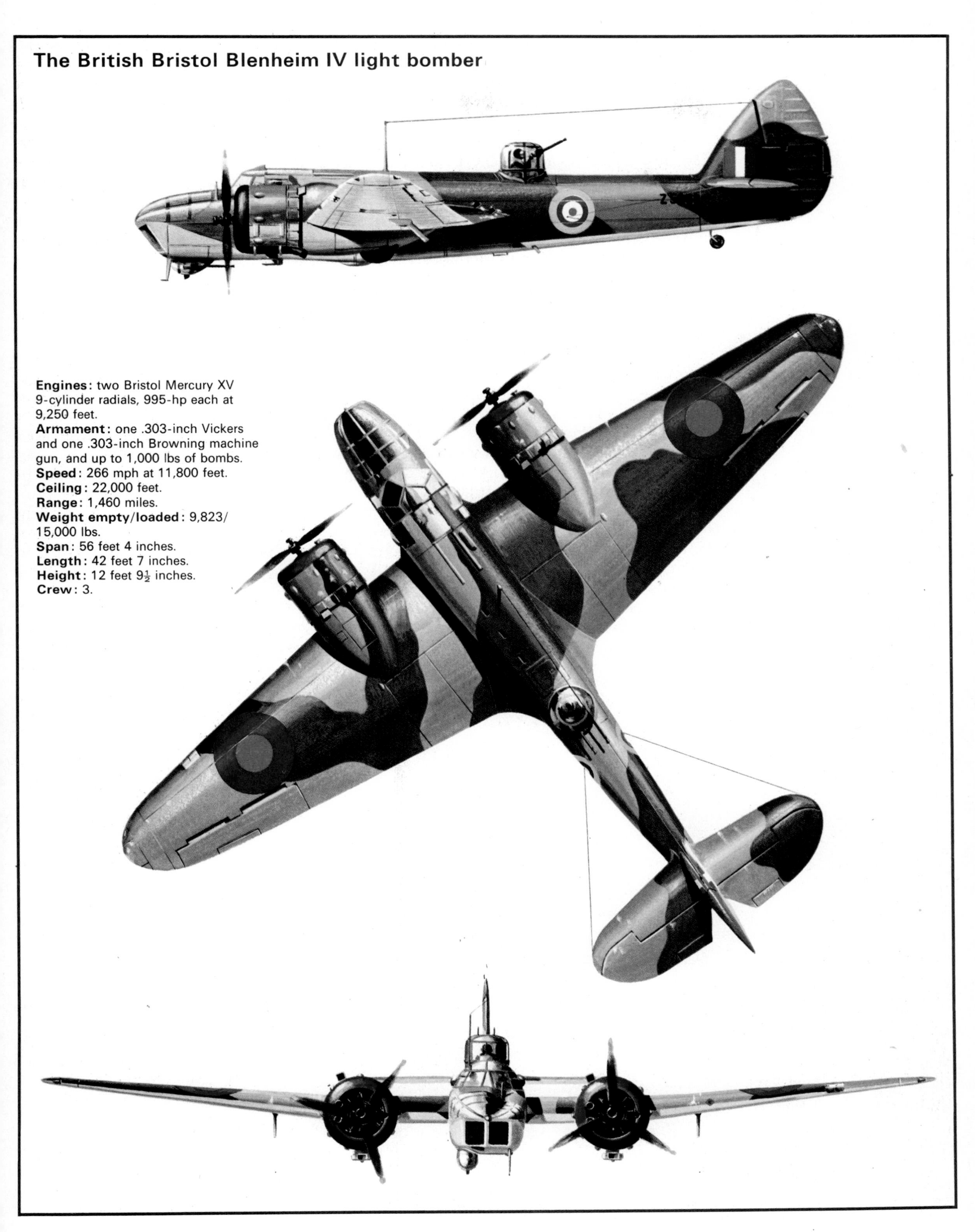
The British Bristol Blenheim IV light bomber
Engines: two Bristol Mercury XV 9-cylinder radials, 995-hp each at 9,250 feet.
Armament: one .303-inch Vickers and one .303-inch Browning machine gun, and up to 1,000 lbs of bombs.
Speed: 266 mph at 11,800 feet.
Ceiling: 22,000 feet.
Range: 1,460 miles.
Weight empty/loaded: 9,823/15,000 lbs.
Span: 56 feet 4 inches.
Length: 42 feet 7 inches.
Height: 12 feet 9½ inches.
Crew: 3.

execution of which was entrusted to Rear-Admiral H. T. Baillie-Grohman. The Australians and New Zealanders left Attica from the little ports of Rafina, Pórto Ráfti and Mégara.

But on April 25, while a detachment of German paratroops was landing on the south bank of the Corinth Canal, the *Leibstandarte*, which had reached Náupaktos, was crossing the Gulf of Patras in makeshift craft and pouring out on to the roads in the Peloponnese. The British Expeditionary Force nevertheless managed to reach the open sea through the ports of Náuplion, Monemvasía (formerly Malvoisia) and Kalamáta.

In all, at the cost of four transports and two destroyers sunk by Stukas, Baillie-Grohman miraculously managed to re-embark 50,732 British, Australian and New Zealand troops.

Maitland Wilson's losses in this rapid and disastrous campaign were 12,712 killed, wounded and missing, including 9,000 prisoners, two-thirds of whom had been swept into the bag around Kalamáta. The Greeks, after a campaign lasting six months, had lost 15,700 killed and missing; 218,000 were taken prisoner by the Germans but these, apart from the officers, were released shortly afterwards.

On May 1 Hitler had good reason to gloat on the rostrum in the Reichstag. He had overrun Yugoslavia and Greece and, for the second time, had driven the British off the continent; and all this in 25 days of fighting and with losses of only 1,684 killed and 3,752 wounded–the equivalent, that is, of one third of one of the 24 divisions he had put into the campaign.

Mussolini, as can be realised, had less reason to boast. He took good care not to publish his losses at the time. But according to the statistics diligently compiled after the war by the historical service of the Italian Army we know that they amounted to more than 102,000 men. There were 13,755 killed, 50,874 wounded and 25,067 missing, most of whom were dead. To make up the total given above 12,368 cases of severe frost-bite must be added. No comment is needed on the desperate state in which the Duce's pseudo-military régime had left the man at the front.

The "New Order" in the Balkans

Victors of the hour, the Führer and the Duce set up the "New Order" in the

▽ *The burnt-out wreck of the British troop transport* Ulster Prince *at Náuplion–one of the several small harbours in southern Greece from which the B.E.F. was evacuated.*
▷ △ *The Greek High Command surrenders to Field-Marshal List.*
▷ ▽ *British prisoners-of-war on a Greek quayside.*

Balkan peninsula and brought in Hungary and Bulgaria to share the spoils of conquest.

Yugoslavia was forthwith dismembered. Slovenia was divided between Germany and Italy, which also took a large slice of the Dalmatian coast and the bay of Kotor. Montenegro got back her independence. Hungary got Bačka, north-west of Belgrade, and Bulgaria got Serbian Macedonia as far as Lake Ohrida, on whose shores King Boris's occupation troops found themselves at daggers drawn with those of his father-in-law, Victor Emmanuel III, King of Italy and Albania.

Mussolini and Ciano set up a Kingdom of Croatia into which they incorporated, quite illegally, the Serbian provinces of Bosnia and Hercegovina. The crown of this puppet state was handed by its new masters in Zagreb to Aymon, Duke of Spoleto, of the House of Savoy. But the new sovereign preferred the society of Rome to the company of General Kvater-

General Ioannis Metaxas was born in 1871. He saw service in the Greco-Turkish War of 1897 before going to Germany for higher training. On the General Staff during the Balkan Wars in 1912, he was appointed Chief-of-Staff in 1913. He advocated neutrality in World War I and went into exile with King Constantine from 1917 to 1921. He was a minister in 1928 but was then in opposition until the monarchy of George II was restored, when he became the Prime Minister and virtual dictator. His régime, efficient but repressive, was largely responsible for Greece's initial survival.

▵ *Greek battleship* Kilkís, *sunk by Luftwaffe bombs in Salamis.* Kilkís *was a tired old pre-Dreadnought which had started life as the U.S.S.* Idaho *before the U.S.A. sold her to Greece in 1914. Part of the deal was the U.S.S.* Mississippi, *which became the* Límnos. *These two old ships had four 12-inch guns, eight 8-inch guns, and eight 7-inch guns. Both were sunk on the same day–April 10, 1941.*

nik and Dr. Ante Pavelić and never set foot in his capital.

From what was left of Greece the conquerors took western Thrace, which, under the promises made by Hitler and Mussolini to King Boris, was awarded to Bulgaria, thus restoring her access to the Aegean, lost under the Treaty of Neuilly in 1919.

All these many alterations to the map of the Balkans were accompanied by frightful atrocities. In Bosnia and Hercegovina the Ustase, as Ante Pavelić's militiamen were called, massacred whole villages of Orthodox and Muslim believers. In Bačka the brutal excesses of the Hungarian troops moved Horthy, the Regent, to indignation, but he was powerless to intervene as the authors of these atrocities claimed to be carrying out the orders of Hitler and Himmler. In their new provinces the Bulgars seemed to have exceeded the Hungarians and equalled the Croats in their savagery.

CHAPTER 36

Assault on Crete

ΔΔ *Artist's impression of the attack on the British cruiser* York *in Suda Bay, Crete, by Italian explosive motor-boats on the morning of March 26, 1941.* York *was badly damaged and had to be beached. Salvage operations had to be abandoned because of subsequent bomb damage, and the battered cruiser* (above) *became an Axis trophy when the Germans took Crete in May that year.*

With Greece evacuated, should the Allies have continued to cling on to Crete? British critics of Churchill's war strategy have said on more than one occasion that the island should have been abandoned. Yet a glance at the map will show that whereas Crete is 500 miles from Alexandria, it is only 200 from Tobruk. Tobruk, the bastion of British resistance in the Middle East, could only be supplied by sea and the great danger was that it might be starved out if the Luftwaffe controlled the aerodromes at Máleme and Heraklion. If Churchill is to be criticised for wanting to fight the war on every front with insufficient means, this is not a front which should be held against him.

Hitler drew similar conclusions. His aims were defensive as well as offensive. Within a few weeks the unleashing of "Barbarossa" would deprive him (only temporarily he hoped) of Russian oil. What would happen if the R.A.F. on Crete were to wipe out all the production of Ploieşti? That is why, on April 25, 1941, his Directive No. 28 ordered the three armies in Greece to prepare Operation "Mercury", which was to secure Crete for Germany.

Brauchitsch, Göring, and Raeder set to work with great energy. And it was no

The German airborne troops and paratroops (Fallschirmjäger) *had an almost unbroken run of success behind them when they were given the task of spearheading the attack on Crete in May 1941. During the assault in the West in the previous year their exploits at Fort Eben-Emaël and elsewhere gave birth to wild rumours of "German parachutists" (as often as not disguised as nuns) descending to wreak havoc in the Allied rear areas. They were brave, tough, well-equipped, and had developed an* esprit *second to none. But the German airborne army was never the same after Crete. It was a Pyrrhic victory: German losses were 7,000 out of 22,000, paratroop losses one man out of four killed. At Máleme airfield alone one aircraft in three was lost. Crete was the last major victory by the German airborne army operating in its original rôle, although paratroop units continued to fight as ground forces, most notably at Monte Cassino in 1944.*

△ *Ready to go: boarding a Ju 52 transport in Greece.*

▷ *These three photographs taken during the assault on Crete show the last moments of a crashing Ju 52, shot down while dropping its paratroops.*

▷▷ *Safely down, and getting their bearings before going into action.*

The German Junkers Ju 52/3 mg7e transport aircraft

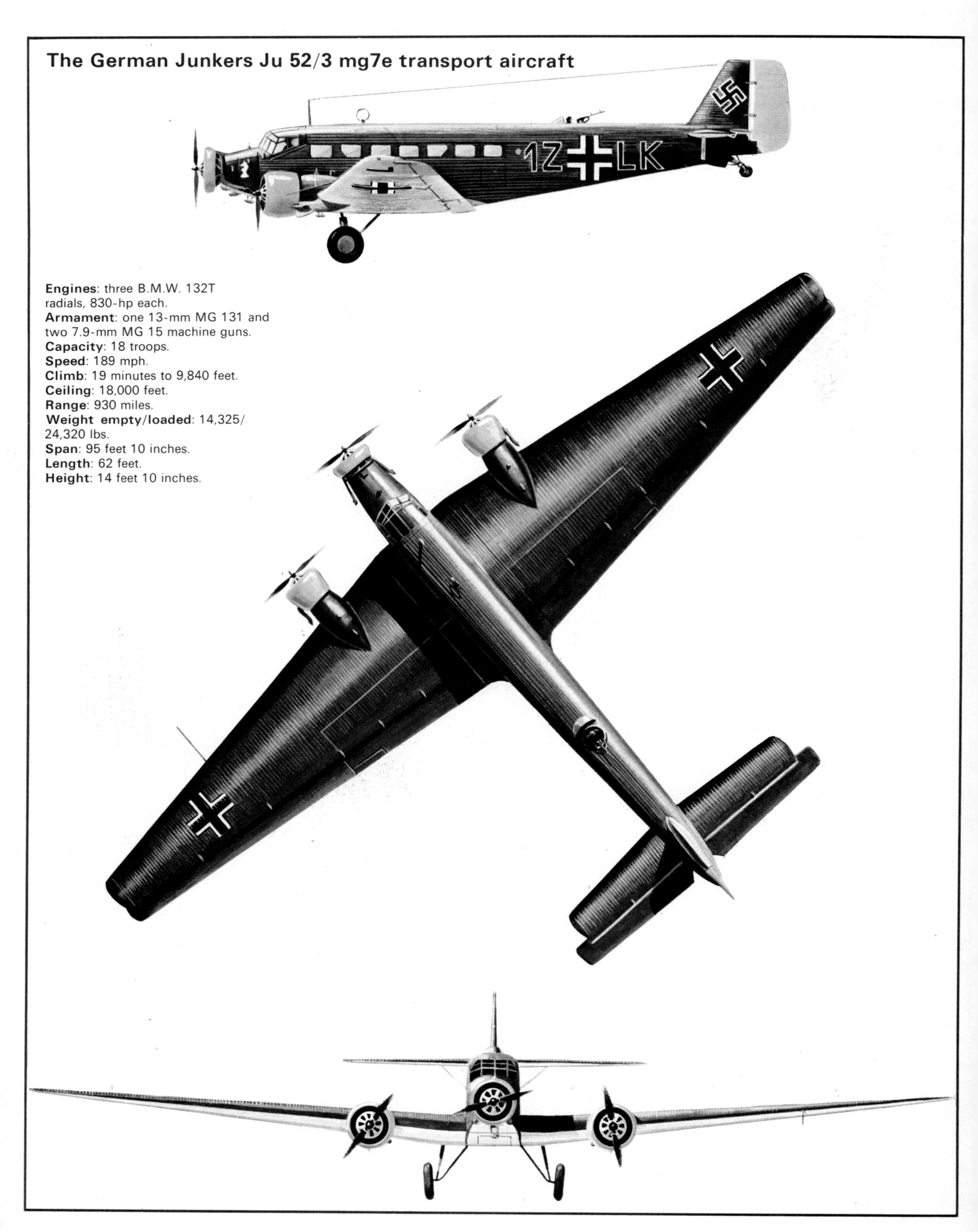

Engines: three B.M.W. 132T radials, 830-hp each.
Armament: one 13-mm MG 131 and two 7.9-mm MG 15 machine guns.
Capacity: 18 troops.
Speed: 189 mph.
Climb: 19 minutes to 9,840 feet.
Ceiling: 18,000 feet.
Range: 930 miles.
Weight empty/loaded: 14,325/24,320 lbs.
Span: 95 feet 10 inches.
Length: 62 feet.
Height: 14 feet 10 inches.

small matter to plan an operation of the size required in a country with such limited resources as Greece where, in particular, air bases had to be improvised.

German preparations

The task of planning the operation fell to General Kurt Student, the commander of XI *Fliegerkorps*, which included the 7th Paratroop Division, reinforced by three infantry regiments from 5th and 6th Mountain Divisions. Air support was to be provided by VIII *Fliegerkorps*, commanded by General Wolfram von Richthofen, 18 fighter and reconnaissance *Gruppen*, that is 228 bombers, 205 dive bombers, 119 single-engined and 114 twin-engined fighters, and 50 reconnaissance aircraft.

The first wave of paratroops was to be carried in 493 three-engined Ju 52's and 72 gliders, but the mountain troops who were to reinforce the paratroops would be ferried over in 63 motorised sailing ships and seven small steamers hastily requisitioned by Rear-Admiral Schuster. This flotilla was to be escorted by two destroy-

△ *A Stuka strike on its way to support the attacking troops. There was no air battle for Crete–the Luftwaffe had things all their own way during the battle because of the decision to evacuate the small R.A.F. forces.*
◁ *Paratroops race into action as another "stick" comes down.*
Overleaf: *German paratroops drift down over Crete–a painting by Grabner.*
Inset overleaf: *The German conquest of Crete. The airborne landings were to have been supported by reinforcements brought in by sea, but the Royal Navy prevented their arrival. Despite their losses, however, the German airborne units proved that they could deal with the conventional forces of the Allies.*

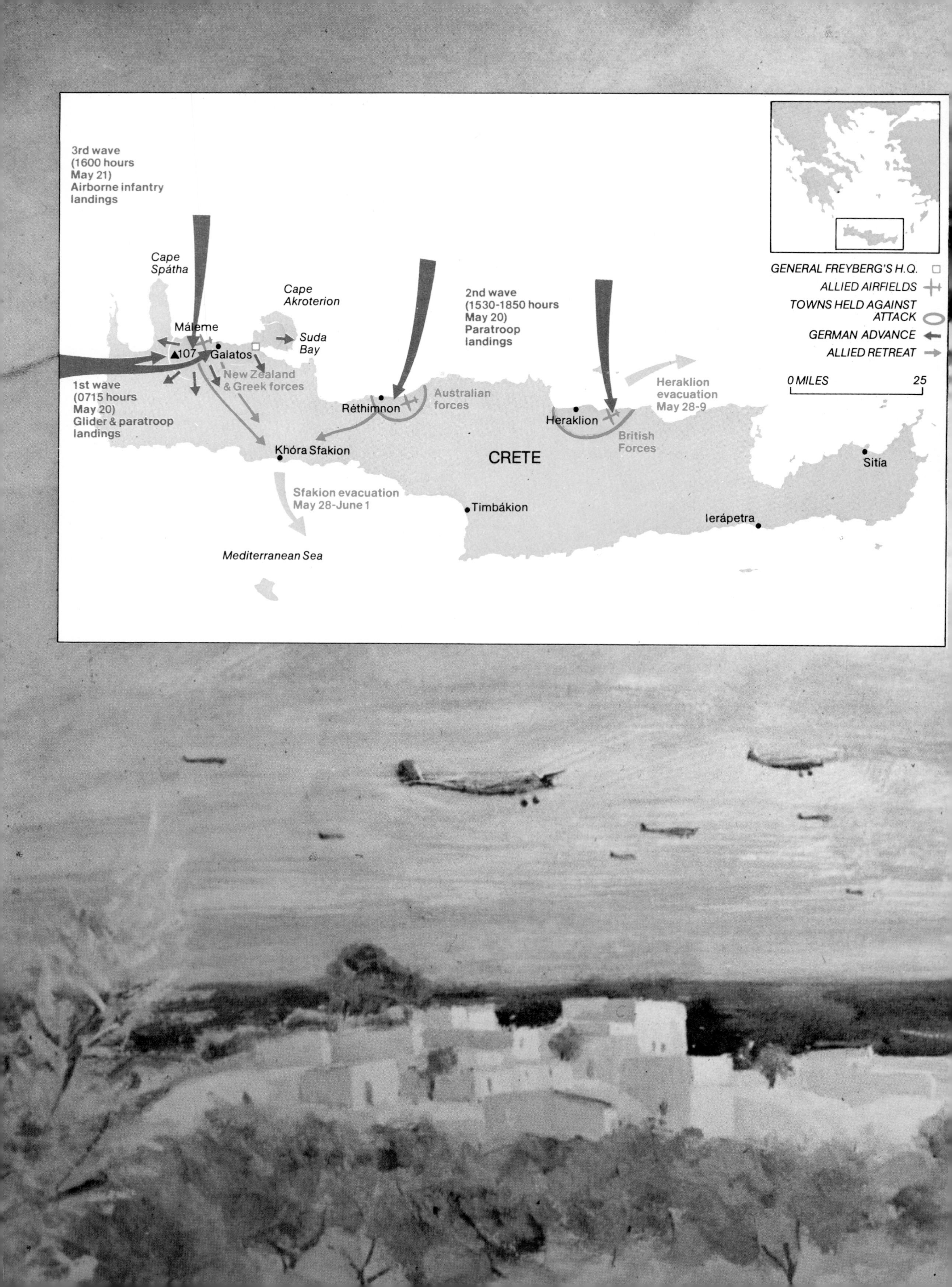
3rd wave
(1600 hours
May 21)
Airborne infantry
landings
Cape
Spátha
Cape
Akroterion
2nd wave
(1530-1850 hours
May 20)
Paratroop
landings
Máleme
▲107
Galatos
Suda
Bay
New Zealand
& Greek forces
1st wave
(0715 hours
May 20)
Glider & paratroop
landings
Réthimnon
Australian
forces
Heraklion
evacuation
May 28-9
Heraklion
British
Forces
Khóra Sfakion
CRETE
Sitía
Sfakion evacuation
May 28-June 1
Timbákion
Ierápetra
Mediterranean Sea
GENERAL FREYBERG'S H.Q.
ALLIED AIRFIELDS
TOWNS HELD AGAINST
ATTACK
GERMAN ADVANCE
ALLIED RETREAT
0 MILES
25

ers and 12 torpedo-boats of the Italian Navy under Captain Peccori-Giraldi.

The defence of Crete

On the island itself, the defence on paper comprised 42,500 men, of whom 10,300 were Greeks. Its core was the A.N.Z.A.C. force, 6,540 Australians and 7,700 New Zealanders who had escaped from Greece but had had to abandon a great deal of material on the beaches of Attica and the Peloponnese. They were thus very short of vehicles, artillery, infantry weapons, ammunition, entrenching tools, barbed wire, blankets, and mess-tins, and were likely to remain so. They had only 68 heavy and light A.A. guns, which were clearly not enough to cover the 162-mile front from the eastern to the western end of the island. On May 1, 1941, the R.A.F. had 35 operational aircraft; on the 19th, after incessant bombardment by the Luftwaffe, it had only four Hurricanes and three Gladiators left in a state good enough to take off for Egypt. Abandoned aerodromes were merely obstructed and not put out of use, as it was intended to reoccupy them as soon as possible.

On April 30, Sir Archibald Wavell entrusted the command of this severely weakened defence force to General Freyberg. Whatever the eminent qualities of this commander, whose 27 wounds testified to his bravery in World War I, he was nevertheless the seventh British commander the island had had in six months and, when he arrived, he had only three weeks in which to familiarise himself with the situation.

Operation "Tiger", which had brought 238 tanks across the Mediterranean, had given the Admiralty the chance of reinforcing the Alexandria naval squadron with the battleship *Queen Elizabeth* and the cruisers *Fiji* and *Naiad*. London thought that this naval force would thus be in a better position to oppose Axis landings on the island from the continent. But Cunningham's only aircraft-carrier, the *Formidable*, had only a handful of Fulmar fighters which, even if there had been more of them, would have been no match for the Germans' Messerschmitts.

▽ Focal point of the assault on Crete: Máleme airfield, where the battle hung in the balance until the defenders were forced back from the perimeter. This picture shows the litter of wrecked and damaged Ju 52's on the airfield–by the end of the battle there were 80 of them. The Germans used a captured British tank to bulldoze the wrecks off the single runway. Allied shells can be seen bursting on the left of the picture.

△ New Zealand recruiting poster. Freyberg's New Zealanders fought superbly–but their courage was not enough to overcome the Germans' determination to gain a foothold on Crete at any cost.
◁ Through the wire . . .
▷ ▽ German forces prepare to embark in the cockleshell armada hastily gathered by Rear-Admiral Schuster for the invasion of Crete, the last bastion of Greece's defence.

German paratroops land

Throughout May 20 airborne troops from the 7th *Fliegerdivision* were dropped at Máleme, west of Canea, and in the areas of Réthimnon and Heraklion. The defenders had been expecting them for 48 hours and so the fighting was bitter. At Máleme General Meindl, gravely wounded, had to hand over his command to Colonel Ramcke; at Réthimnon the paratroops landed with no commander at all as the glider carrying General Sussman had crashed on the island of Aegina. The battle might have swung in General Freyberg's favour had he had time to reinforce the brigade defending Máleme airstrip against Ramcke, and if the Mediterranean Fleet had been able to destroy completely the convoys bringing in Lieutenant-General Ringel's mountain troops. But, for the few losses they inflicted on the Germans, the Royal Navy lost, in rapid succession from aerial bombardment by Stukas, the cruisers *Gloucester* and *Fiji* together with four destroyers, while the *Warspite* and the aircraft-carrier *Formidable* were so badly damaged that they had to be sent for repair in the United States.

In spite of pressure from London, Admiral Cunningham had to give up operations north of Crete, where he was suffering heavy losses. On May 25, with admirably controlled air support, the 5th Mountain Division managed to break out of the Máleme perimeter held by the 2nd New Zealand Division and push on through Canea. The German breakthrough decided General Freyberg on May 27 to begin the evacuation of the island and to ask for help from the Mediterranean Fleet. This help was not refused him.

The evacuation of Crete

In spite of the risks involved and the losses already sustained, the Commander-in-Chief Mediterranean, Admiral Cunningham, did not hesitate a moment.

"We cannot let [the army] down," he signalled to the ships of his fleet which had been designated for this mission, and when one member of his staff seemed pessimistic he retorted, with a just sense of realities: "It takes the Navy three years to build a ship. It would take 300 years to re-build a tradition."

The evacuation of Crete, begun on the night of May 28–29, was carried out through the small harbour at Sphakia on the south coast and was completed by dawn on June 2. During the operation the A.A. cruiser *Calcutta* and the destroyers *Hereward* and *Imperial* were lost. But the heaviest losses of life were on board the cruiser *Orion*, Vice-Admiral Pridham-Wippell's flagship. One single German bomb killed 260 men and wounded 280.

Altogether 4,704 out of 7,700 New Zealanders and 3,164 out of 6,540 Australians landed at Alexandria, but of these 1,464 were wounded. About 8,800 out of 17,000 British were also evacuated. But the losses of General Student and XI *Fliegerkorps* had not been slight in spite of this. Though the Germans' casualties could not have reached the 15,000 given by Churchill in his memoirs, statistics published since the war show that, with 3,714 killed and missing and 2,494 wounded, the eight days of fighting on Crete had cost the Germans more than the whole three

◁ For the victors – time out for a quick cigarette and a drink.
◁ ▽ German mountain troops, hastily flown in to bolster the hard-pressed airborne units, establish themselves in the hills.
▽ Paratroops move forward under the cover of a gully. "A few land mines and booby-traps would soon account for this little bunch," boasts the British wartime caption for this picture. It was wishful thinking.

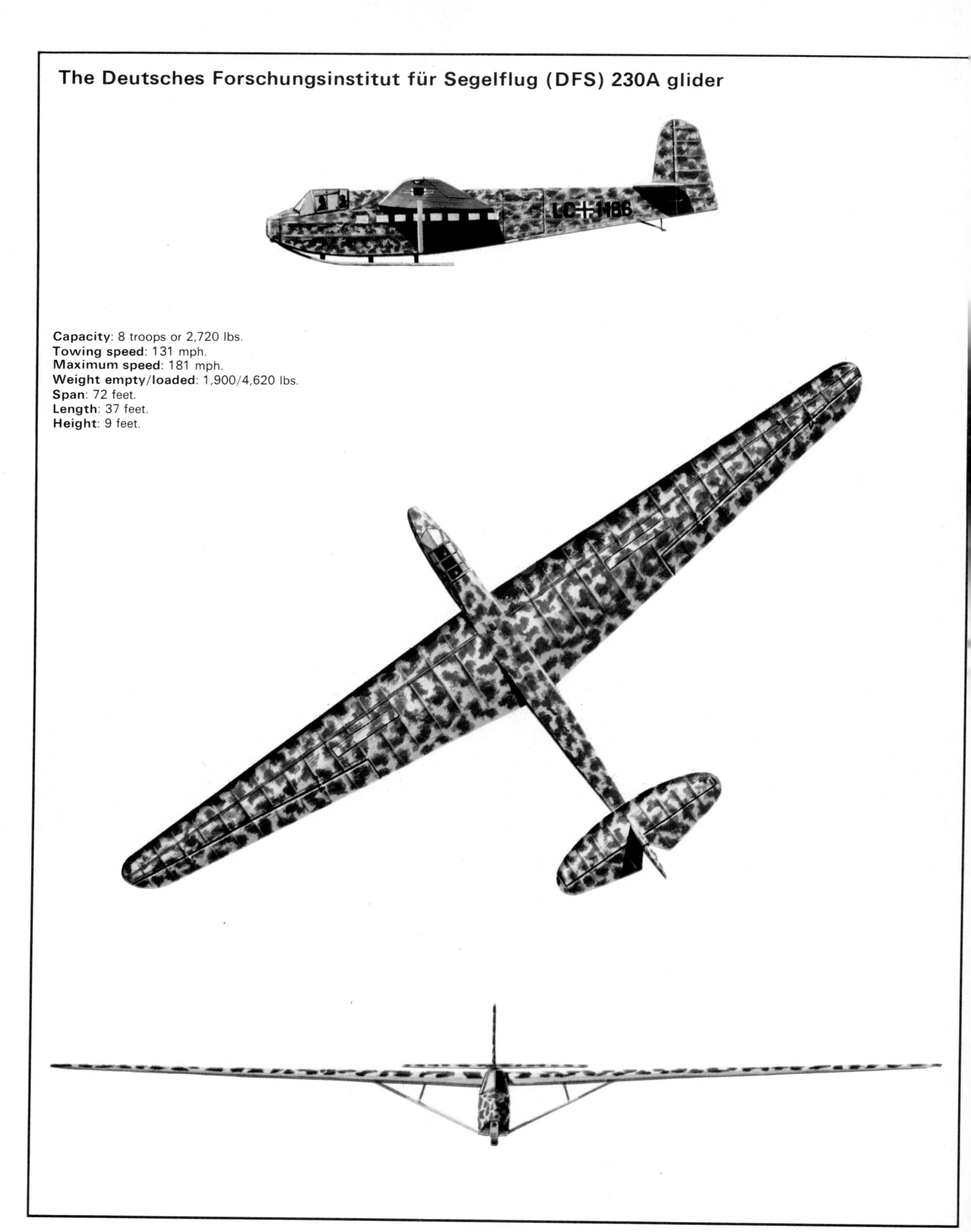

The Deutsches Forschungsinstitut für Segelflug (DFS) 230A glider

Capacity: 8 troops or 2,720 lbs.
Towing speed: 131 mph.
Maximum speed: 181 mph.
Weight empty/loaded: 1,900/4,620 lbs.
Span: 72 feet.
Length: 37 feet.
Height: 9 feet.

weeks of the Balkans campaign. The Royal Navy lost 2,011 officers and men.

Was it because of these German losses that Hitler rejected General Student's suggestion to follow up the victory on Crete by capturing Cyprus? We do not know. But the memory of this blood-bath admittedly encouraged Hitler to abandon his operation "Hercules" (the capture of Malta from the air) in late June 1942, when Rommel thought he had convinced him that the Axis forces could get to the Nile and Suez. In any case, the British forces in Libya, in Macedonia, and in the Aegean Sea had suffered heavy reverses which more than balanced the losses accountable to Italian strategy in the previous winter. Did the War Cabinet's decisions and the orders of the Imperial General Staff "lamentably" fail to appreciate the situation, as Lord Cunningham of Hyndhope claims in his *A Sailor's Odyssey*? It is difficult to dispute the validity of this statement by one of the great commanders of the war, yet in the end, we cannot always do as we would wish in war and sometimes the only choice left lies between two very great disadvantages. Churchill's solution was not necessarily the wrong one, therefore. Fifteen years of disarmament had reduced Britain to this level of impotence.

▵ ▵ After the defeat of Crete the British used this picture of Germans questioning a Cretan village headman for propaganda purposes. "Their brutal faces press round him as they demand information. This can happen here . . ."

◃ and ▵ Rounding up the prisoners. British and Empire P.O.W.s taken on Crete totalled 11,835.

CHAPTER 37
Russia's time runs out

When Hitler decided to take on the Soviet Union and destroy Stalin and his régime it was not because, like Napoleon, he had faced up to the impossibility of getting his armies across the Channel. He had already come to this decision as far back as June 29, 1940, at a time, that is, when preparations for Operation "Sea Lion" were just getting under way.

During the "phoney war", under the Moscow treaties of August 23 and September 28, 1939, the two totalitarian powers had continued to give each other discreet but very valuable assistance.

But the agreement on the economic conditions of the Soviet-German Pact was not signed until February 11, 1940, after negotiations which had lasted throughout the autumn of 1939. The Russian delegation had been led by Molotov and Mikoyan, two very touchy and obdurate bargainers. In addition to the material provided for in August 1939 and now in the course of being delivered, the Soviet Union undertook to supply to the Reich between then and August 11, 1941 some 650 million marks' worth of raw materials and foodstuffs.

In exchange for these products, the Reich was to supply to the Soviet Union military material, as well as equipment, machinery, and plant for heavy industry. Moscow's negotiators were particularly interested in the production of synthetic petrol by the hydrogenation of coal and in the manufacture of synthetic rubber, called *Buna*, two processes which had been perfected in Germany.

In the supply of arms, Joseph Stalin's concern was chiefly for his navy. He asked for the uncompleted heavy cruiser *Lützow*, the plans for the battleship *Bismarck*, and for a destroyer armed with 6-inch guns, a complete 15-inch gun turret, designs for 11- and 16-inch turrets, and specimens of engine parts, torpedoes, magnetic mines, and periscopes. Then came demands for the delivery of some samples of certain army and air force material: Pzkw III tanks, all-purpose transport vehicles, 21-cm howitzers, 10.5-cm A.A. guns, Messerschmitt 109 and 110 fighters, Junkers 88 bombers, and plant for the production of explosives and ammunition.

The German delegation had to accept these demands. But, on Hitler's orders, the German war industry, already overstretched, showed no great alacrity in supplying these orders. In fact only the cruiser *Lützow* was handed over to the Soviet Union and she was uncompleted and remained so. The Soviet delegation in Berlin entrusted with seeing to the delivery of this material was not taken in by the delays, and a certain tension thus crept into the relations between the two capitals.

Russia approves of *Weserübung*

On April 9 the weather had suddenly turned fine in the Kremlin. When Schulenburg, the German Ambassador, told him of the measures which the Reich was taking against Denmark and Norway, Molotov readily agreed that Germany had had no alternative and, according to the Ambassador, he said "literally": "We wish Germany complete success in these defensive measures."

Was the People's Commissar for Foreign Affairs putting a good face on things? This was not Schulenburg's impression, and he was a very acute observer. In his despatch of April 11 he noted that in reply to Berlin's complaints about the temporary suspension of grain and oil deliveries, Molotov had been "affability itself" and had attributed these and other annoyances to "over-zealous minions".

Russian deliveries to Germany were resumed quickly and on May 10, 1940, the German Ambassador in Moscow, who had been instructed to inform Molotov of the invasion of Belgium, the Netherlands, and France, was able to telegraph his government: "Instruction *re* Molotov carried out. Molotov received communication in spirit of understanding, adding that he realised that Germany had to protect herself against Franco-British attack. He does not doubt our success."

The same tune again on June 18. On that day Molotov summoned Count von der Schulenburg to his office to explain to

◁ *Joseph Stalin, effective dictator of the Soviet Union. How would he react to the obvious implications of Germany's conquest of the Balkans?*

▽ *German comment when the gloves came off and the gushing expressions of mutual friendship died away*–from Lustige Blätter.

△ *Count Friedrich von der Schulenburg, Germany's astute and capable Ambassador in Moscow.*

▽ *Important pawn for Hitler: the Rumanian oil wells at Ploieşti. Fears of Allied air strikes at Ploieşti from bases on Crete had played a substantial part in the decision to reduce the island. Another reason for Hitler's obsession with Ploieşti was the fact that any attack on the Soviet Union would cut off Germany's supplies of Russian oil . . .*

him what measures the Soviet Union had taken against the Baltic countries. But before he broached the subject, he wished to offer "his government's warmest congratulations on the splendid success of the German armed forces".

Molotov's remarks on the German armed intervention were accepted calmly by the Count, who was acting on instructions circulated by telegraph to all Heads of Missions of the Third Reich on the previous day by the Secretary of State for Foreign Affairs, Baron von Weizsäcker. This instruction ordered that Russia and the Baltic States should be left alone to work out the problem of their "co-operation".

The rape of Bessarabia

At the Munich conference on June 19, 1940, the Führer spoke in similar terms to Count Ciano about the "incorporation" of Estonia, Latvia, and Lithuania into the Soviet Union. According to him it was a "natural and inevitable" event and, from their conversations on the subject, Ciano got the impression that Hitler was "not then contemplating action against Russia".

Eight days later the Kremlin sent a strongly-worded ultimatum to the Rumanian Government demanding that it should give up Bessarabia and Bukovina within 48 hours. In the secret protocol to the Soviet-German Non-Aggression Pact, the Reich had stated that it was totally unconcerned with the former province. But Bukovina was not mentioned in the pact and, as Berlin remarked, it had never been part of the Czarist Russian Empire.

Not wishing, however, to see war break out between the Dniestr and the Prut at a time when they thought they had halted it on the continent, Hitler and Mussolini reacted energetically, urging unquestioning acceptance of the Russian terms on Bucharest. In Moscow, Schulenburg, accepting the *fait accompli* in Bessarabia, merely drew attention to the fate in Bukovina of the 100,000 *Volkdeutschen* who lived there. But, in his triumphal speech to the Reichstag on July 17, the Führer proclaimed *urbi et orbi:* "The agreement signed in Moscow between the Reich and the Soviet Union has established precisely once and for all their respective areas of influence. Neither Germany nor Russia has so far set a single foot outside these areas." And so the most authoritative voice of the Third Reich made his partner's invasions of Finland, the Baltic States, and Rumania seem part of the Soviet-German Pact.

Was Hitler lying when he made this solemn declaration? Perhaps so, for he had ordered the transfer to the Eastern Front from July 20 onwards of the 18th Army (Colonel-General von Küchler), six corps strong: in all 15 infantry divisions and the 1st Cavalry Division. Yet there may have been good reason for this, as the German troops were very thin on the ground between the Carpathians and the

△ *Poring over maps, the Axis leaders play Napoleon for the camera. At the Führer's elbow hovers General Jodl of O.K.W.; the ever-present Field-Marshal Keitel presides in the background.*

Baltic, looking more like a series of customs posts, in face of the massive Russian occupying forces, than a strategically deployed army, albeit on the defensive. It was natural, therefore, that he should wish to thicken up the line. On the other hand, in the same period O.K.H. was ordered to reduce its strength from 155 to 120 divisions, though the latter included, it is true, 20 armoured and ten motorised divisions.

Hitler's decision to attack the Soviet Union can therefore be pinpointed to his stay in Berchtesgaden between July 20 and 29, 1940. It arose from a kind of inspired insight after a long period of solitary meditation. Even today it is difficult to see what processes of thought led him to this conclusion. It is reasonable to suppose that the presence of Soviet bombers within 30 minutes' flying time of the indispensable Ploiesti oil fields had a great deal to do with his decision. At the very least one might say that the rape of Bessarabia crystallised his inclinations towards aggression and brought him back to the ideology of *Mein Kampf*, which he had somewhat neglected since August 23, 1939.

However this may be, as described above, on July 29 General of Artillery Jodl came down from Berchtesgaden at the end of the day and gathered together his most important colleagues of the *Wehrmachtsführungsamt* (Armed Forces Operational Staff): Colonel Warlimont, Lieutenant-Colonel von Lossberg, Lieutenant-Commander Junge, and Major von Falkenstein of the Luftwaffe. They met in his Command H.Q. train, the *Atlas*, halted in Bad Reichenhall station and, enjoining on the others the strictest secrecy, Jodl revealed the Führer's determination to crush the Soviet Union.

"Hitler," Keitel said at Nuremberg, "wanted to know if something could be done immediately. The generals said 'no'. War against Russia simply could not be entertained in the autumn of 1940."

To have the army fight in Poland, transport it to the west to fight again, and then return it to Poland to fight once more was absolutely impossible. The troops needed to be re-equipped.

"But the question he asked was a fair indication of the workings of his mind. 'I was worried,' said Warlimont. 'I was worried,' said Jodl. 'I was worried,' said Keitel."

▽ *Field-Marshal List, the man who conquered the Balkans for Hitler–and by so doing secured Germany's southern flank for any subsequent moves against Soviet Russia.*

Hitler's war plan

Hitler forestalled the objections he expected from those who counselled a prudent conduct of the war: would this not be reviving the risk of war on two fronts which had brought Imperial Germany to her final defeat in 1918 and which the Non-Aggression Pact of 1939 had so opportunely eliminated? To this he replied that he would be eliminating Great Britain's last possible continental ally and this would be done before the intervention of the United States in 1942 or 1943. From then onwards Russia would be crushed for ever.

Two days later, on July 31, Grand-Admiral Raeder and *Reichsmarschall* Göring, with their Chiefs-of-Staff, went up to the Berghof where Hitler told them of his decision: to his great regret an attack in the autumn was out of the question; the operation would therefore begin in May 1941. He saw the offensive developing as two main thrusts: one towards Kiev, the other towards Moscow.

Russia's organised forces were to be crushed within five months. The operation was subsequently to allow the rapid occupation of the Baku oilfields.

Halder's diary, normally so incisive as far as Hitler is concerned, records on this date no fundamental objection to the proposed operation. It is true that the principle of it was not discussed, but the impromptu decision which had been taken nevertheless brought the German High Command up against problems which it would be difficult to solve within the prescribed time.

As Britain was to be defeated by sea and air, the High Command had been called upon to demobilise or to send on leave 35 divisions. Hitler's oracular pronouncement required the army to be increased to 180 divisions, the number of Panzer divisions to be doubled, and the large motorised formations to be increased from four to six. This meant the creation of some 40 divisions, plus the corps troops and H.Q.s to support and staff them. At the same time, the planning of the operation against the Soviet Union was entrusted to Major-General Marcks, who was replaced on September 3, 1940 by Lieutenant-General Paulus, then Deputy Chief of General Staff.

German-Soviet relations grow sour

If even now Hitler had yet to make his final decision, a series of incidents arising from fortuitous circumstances caused German-Soviet relations to become further embittered. There was firstly the settlement at Vienna. When they had settled the conflict between Hungary and Rumania over Transylvania, neither Hitler nor Mussolini had intended to trick the Soviets. Nevertheless, to sweeten the bitter pill being offered to King Carol, Germany and Italy had to promise him their guarantee for what was left of his kingdom. Instructed to inform Molotov of the solution reached at the Belvedere Palace, Count von der Schulenburg had to put it to him that the two Axis powers had acted solely in the interests of peace and that the Reich still valued the friendship of the Russians as highly as ever.

Despite the placatory aspect of the account, Molotov retorted that he had only heard of the Vienna settlement through the newspapers and that, by keeping him in ignorance of the matter, the Reich had contravened Article 3 of the Non-Aggression Pact, which obliged both parties to consult each other. On the other hand, according to Grigore Gafencu, then Rumania's representative in Moscow, Molotov is said to have asked: "Why did you give this guarantee? You had been advised that we had no intention of attacking Rumania." To this Schulenburg replied, with some presence of mind: "That is precisely why we gave it. You had told us that you had no claims on that country; our guarantee could not therefore embarrass you in any way."

The signature on September 27, 1940 of

the Tripartite Pact between Berlin, Rome, and Tokyo also provoked requests for explanations from Moscow. The German Foreign Ministry claimed the pact was purely defensive and intended by the three powers to dissuade Washington from poaching upon the preserves of Germany in Europe and Africa, and of Japan in China and South-East Asia. But the Kremlin wondered if this public instrument aimed at American "warmongers" did not contain, as did the Soviet-German Pact of August 23, 1939, some more sinister secret protocol.

Another cause for alarm was Germany's receipt from Sweden and Finland, in September 1940, of permission to transport artillery through their territory for the reinforcement of Norway's arctic defences. At this period Soviet-Finnish relations were becoming daily more tense on account of the Soviet Union's abusive interpretations of the peace treaty of the previous March 12. Was Germany going to interfere in this wolf-lamb dialogue?

Finally, the announcement that a German military mission accompanied by "demonstration troops" was about to undertake the training of the Rumanian Army caused no pleasure to the Soviets, who were attempting to increase their presence in the Danube delta, in the southern part of Bessarabia.

In the face of this persistent ill-humour and of the risk of seeing the Soviet Union suspend its deliveries of raw materials, Ribbentrop, acting on Hitler's orders, sent a long letter to Stalin on October 13. It took up the complaints made by Moscow, but in particular pointed out to Stalin the conclusion that "the four great powers, the U.S.S.R., Italy, Japan, and Germany, had the historic mission of adopting a long-term policy and guiding the future development of their peoples in the directions determined by the worldwide boundaries of their interests."

To this effect he suggested that Stalin send Molotov to Berlin. He would be welcome there and this would give the Führer an opportunity to explain his concept of future Soviet-German relations.

Was Ribbentrop trying to deceive Stalin, offering to enlarge on his behalf the concept of the tripartite system, while the German High Command was setting up Operation "Barbarossa", designed to bring about the final destruction of the Soviet state and government? It would rather seem that before deciding irrevocably, the leaders of the Third Reich wished to know the Kremlin's intentions about sharing out the planet. If Molotov accepted the delimitation of the spheres of interest proposed by Hitler and Ribbentrop the projected campaign might be unnecessary; otherwise it would be war.

On October 22 Stalin replied to Ribben-

△ King Carol II of Rumania with his son, Crown Prince Michael. His attempts to govern Rumania the way Hitler wanted led first to his own expulsion by the right wing "Iron Guard", and then to the German takeover in April 1941.

△ *A sign of the times: General Stanzer, commander of the puppet state of Croatia's armed forces, inspects a piece of artillery during a visit to a Bosnian regiment. Such forces were of little real use to the Axis, however, except for police duties in the Balkans.*

trop by letter, agreeing with his long-term proposals and delimiting the spheres of influence to be shared between Germany and the Soviet Union. Consequently Molotov would go to Berlin at a date to be fixed between November 10 and 12. Yet in September Field-Marshals von Bock, von Kluge, and List and the H.Q.s of Army Group "B" and the 4th and 12th Armies had already been transferred to the Eastern Front. These comprised four corps. in all ten infantry, one motorised, and three armoured divisions. Soon afterwards Field-Marshal von Leeb and the H.Q. of Army Group "C", stationed at Nancy, were recalled to Germany. On October 30 Field-Marshal von Brauchitsch's staff left its quarters at Fontainebleau to return to the quarters at Zossen Camp, south of Berlin, which they had left on the evening of the previous May 9.

In the evening of November 10 Molotov, accompanied by his deputy, left Moscow for Berlin. On November 12 at Anhalt Station, where Ribbentrop had gone to greet him, all the correct ceremonial was obeyed punctiliously.

Hitler meets Molotov

Molotov had a preliminary conversation with his German colleague in the Foreign Ministry. A few hours later he was received by Hitler, who also gave up the following day to him. On the morning of November 14 Molotov took the train back to Moscow.

We have only the German version of these crucial talks, yet again from Paul Schmidt, as Molotov's conversations with Ribbentrop and Hitler are not even mentioned in the official *History of the Great Patriotic War of the Soviet Union*.

This is discretion indeed. But whatever the reason for the silence, Paul Schmidt's evidence shows that Molotov's conversation with Ribbentrop was limited merely to generalities.

As Germany had by now practically won the war, it was time to proceed to a division of the Old World, and to this effect Ribbentrop recommended that the four totalitarian powers should all drive southwards: Germany and Italy would take over Africa and Japan South-East Asia. This left a large area between the Caspian and Singapore which might without difficulty be allotted to the Soviet Union, giving the Russians an outlet to the open sea in the Persian Gulf and the Indian Ocean. Ribbentrop thus proposed to Molotov a system of four parallel thrusts to the south and, as parallels only meet at infinity, there was no risk in an agreement of this kind of any friction or even of encounter between Japan and the U.S.S.R. in the Far East or between the U.S.S.R. and Germany on the Bosporus or in the Middle East.

Ribbentrop also suggested that an arrangement be made between the three powers of the Tripartite Pact on the one hand and the Soviet Union on the other. By way of encouragement to Molotov, Ribbentrop said that Germany was prepared to replace the Montreux Agreements of 1936, governing the Bosporus and Dardanelles, by a new convention which Turkey would be called upon to negotiate, if that is the word, with Germany, Italy, and Russia. But Molotov took good care not to show his hand. He asked for a few explanations, but all the time gave it to be understood that his principal concern was an agreement between Germany and Russia, and that only after this was concluded would he consent to talk with Italy and Japan. According to Paul Schmidt, Molotov was visibly holding himself back for his meeting with the Führer.

With that peculiar psychological insight which characterised him, Adolf Hitler understood immediately that his usual tactics of intimidation would be of no avail against this old Bolshevik Vyacheslav Skriabin, of excellent Great-Russian bourgeois stock. It was not for nothing that his comrades in the party had nicknamed him the "Hammer" (Molotov). This was Schmidt's observation during these three long and difficult sessions. Peppered with precise questions by the Russian, the Führer contained himself: "He didn't jump into the air and he didn't rush to the door as he had done in September 1939 when Sir Horace Wilson handed him Chamberlain's letter. Nor did he declare that further discussion was useless as he had done three weeks earlier to Franco at Hendaye. He was gentleness and courtesy personified."

But then, moving on from the generalities about the delimitation of spheres of influence and the exclusion of the United States from affairs in Europe, Africa and Asia, it became apparent that any agreement between Germany and Russia on the

▽ The scene in the Belvedere Palace in Vienna as Bulgaria joins the Tripartite Pact.

Baltic Sea
North Sea
Hamburg
Danzig
Bremen
Stettin
The Hague
Bromber
HOLLAND
Hanover
Berlin
Posen
Brussels
Cologne
GERMANY
BELGIUM
Breslau
LUXEMBOURG
Prague
Nuremberg
Nancy
Stuttgart
Strasbourg
SLOVAK
Munich
Bratislava
Vienna
Salzburg
Innsbruck
Berne
FRANCE
SWITZERLAND
Buda
Lyons
HUNGARY
Ljubljana
Milan
Zagreb
Venice
Turin
Genoa
CROATIA
Nice
Florence
Sarajevo
Livorno
ITALY
MONTENEG
Corsica
Mediterranean Sea
Adriatic Sea
Rome
ALB
Sardinia
Naples
Bari
Tir

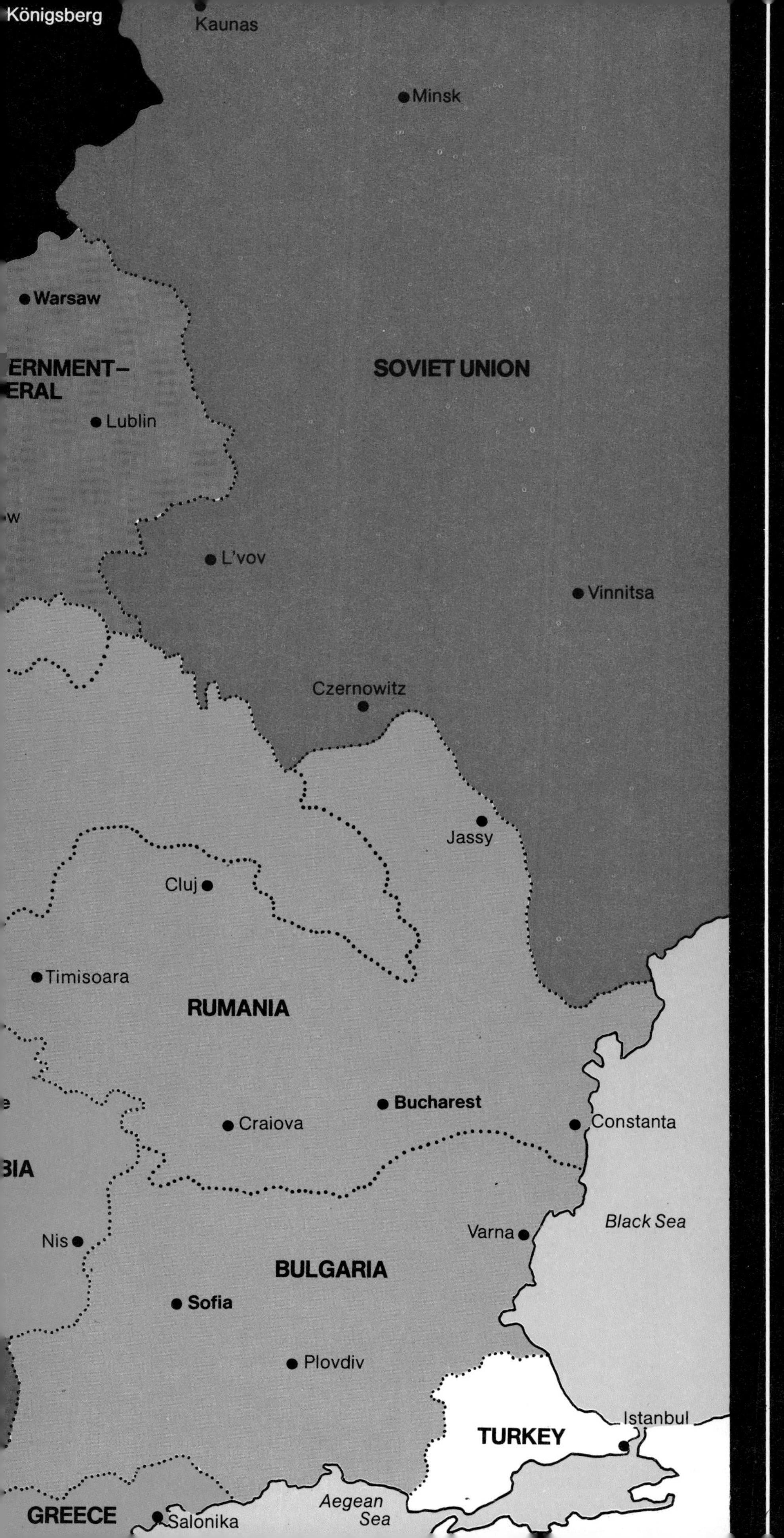

SPRING 1941: THE AXIS STRANGLEHOLD ON EUROPE

After the Balkans/Crete campaign of April-May 1941, Germany's domination of central and south-eastern Europe was complete. Hitler's Reich was flanked on the east and west by securely-occupied territory. To the south-west lay Vichy France, truncated, immobilised, determined, thanks to Pétain's rule, to commit herself neither to the Allies nor to Germany. To the south-east lay Germany's satellites and allies, almost unrecognisably swollen with the territorial annexations made under Hitler's patronage. And to the south lay Italy, saved from humiliating defeat by German intervention, and now joint occupying power in the conquered Balkans.

Hitler and Ribbentrop had used every trick in the book to exploit the territorial grievances left unsatisfied by the Treaty of Versailles. Slovakia had appeared on the map as an "independent" state under German patronage. Hungary and Bulgaria had been fed with choice tit-bits from the former territories of Czechoslovakia, Rumania, Yugoslavia, and Greece. Even in conquered Yugoslavia the Croat-Serb rivalry had been exploited to the full, with Croatia welcoming Axis patronage.

Such was the condition of Europe as the summer of 1941 approached. The Axis was in complete control, massing its troops from the Baltic to the Black Sea for the greatest trial of all: the assault on Soviet Russia.

"When the alarm sounded Ribbentrop led the way down many flights of stairs to a deep shelter sumptuously furnished. When he got inside the raid had begun. He shut the door and said to Molotov: 'Now here we are alone together. Why should we not divide?' Molotov said: 'What will England say?' 'England,' said Ribbentrop, 'is finished. She is no more use as a Power.' 'If that is so,' said Molotov, 'Why are we in this shelter, and whose are these bombs which fall?'

△ △ *November 12, 1940 at the Anhalt Station in Berlin: the German Foreign Minister, Joachim von Ribbentrop (second from left, front row), accompanies his guest and opposite number from the Soviet Union, People's Commissar for Foreign Affairs Vyacheslav Molotov (on Ribbentrop's left) as he inspects the guard of honour.*
◁ *From one ceremony to another. Molotov arrives outside the New Chancellery, the Führer's official residence in Berlin.*

△ *The serious business of the visit gets under way. Molotov and Ribbentrop get down to the talks that ended in an apparent* détente *between the two great European powers. Russia, blind to Germany's real intentions, expressed so forcibly in* Mein Kampf, *believed that the results of the meeting were genuine. Hitler, however, was just playing for time–a few more months and the evil of Communism would be struck a blow which it stood no chance of surviving.*

four points raised by Molotov was impossible:

1. The Soviet Government considered it to be its duty to settle once and for all the Finnish question. "No war in Finland," Hitler protested; "We need peace in Finland because of nickel and wood; a conflict in the Baltic might have unforeseen consequences on Soviet-German relations."
2. Was the disagreeable guarantee given to Rumania also valid against Russia? "Of course," Hitler replied. But he added, in the manner of his Ambassador in Moscow: "This question cannot become serious for you. You reached an agreement with the Rumanians a short time ago."
3. "In that case then," Molotov went on imperturbably, "would Germany agree to Russia's offering similar guarantees to Bulgaria and following them up with a strong military mission?" Hitler answered this question with another: "Has Bulgaria, like Rumania, asked for such a guarantee?" When Molotov replied "no", Hitler said he would have to consult Mussolini before coming to a decision on this matter.
4. Finally they came to the question of the Straits. As far as a guarantee against attack from the Black Sea was concerned, Molotov was not content with a paper revision of the Montreux Agreements. In addition to the security provided by the stationing of Soviet troops in Bulgaria, he also demanded the right to land and naval bases in the Bosporus and Dardanelles areas. Hitler, once again, refused.

German and Soviet aims irreconcilable

And so Germany's attempt to divert Russia's traditional direction of advance, from south-west to south, had failed. As for the rest, it is not that Stalin and Molotov had scorned the prospects offered to them by Hitler and Ribbentrop in the direction of the Persian Gulf, but that they had connected these with their claims on Finland, Bulgaria, and Turkey. This view is supported by the draft agreement drawn up in the Kremlin listing the conditions under which the U.S.S.R. would join the Tripartite Pact. These were submitted to Berlin by Count von der Schulenburg on November 26.

In particular, giving his opinion on the articles of a draft German scheme aimed at revising the terms of the Montreux Agreements, Molotov wrote: "The draft protocol or agreement between Germany, Italy, and the Soviet Union must be amended to guarantee to the latter long-term leases on light naval and land-force bases on the Bosporus and in the Dardanelles. It would guarantee the independence and territorial integrity of Turkey, the guarantee to be signed by the three states mentioned above, were she to express her wish to join the four-party pact. In the case of Turkey's refusal to join with the four powers, the above protocol should envisage the agreement of Germany, Italy, and the Soviet Union to prepare and execute appropriate military and diplomatic procedures. A separate agreement should be concluded to this effect."

Engaged as he was in a struggle to the death with Great Britain, Hitler allowed the conversation to drop. Already the presence in the Balkans of the lone, unfortunate cavalier Mussolini risked the intervention of Britain. An initiative by the Russians against Finland must not give the British an excuse to land at Petsamo. On the other hand, developments on the Albanian front made it seem likely that the Wehrmacht would have to go to the help of the Italian armies by manoeuvring through Bulgaria. In which case how could Russia be allowed the right to set up "strong military missions" in the Bulgarian ports of Varna and Burgas? Finally, the pressure which Molotov wanted him to bring to bear on Turkey might drive the Government of Ankara to open its frontiers to the British forces in the Middle East, the strength of which had given the German High Command some strange illusions.

Molotov did not on this occasion display his normal finesse. In the last analysis he had revealed to Hitler the next objectives of Soviet policy and demonstrated quite clearly that Moscow's and Berlin's theses on the sharing out of the planet were and would remain irreconcilable. On the other hand he left for Moscow without suspecting the alternative with which he had been left. As a matter of fact, the soundings and the feelers he had used on the persons of Hitler and Ribbentrop did not reveal to him that in the event of disagreement with the programme set before him the result would be war. And it was to be a

△ △ *Liberty, Fraternity, and Equality, Russian style, according to the* Lustige Blätter *of Berlin. The Red bear of the secret police sits on the subjected peoples of the Russian empire.*

△ *Again from the* Lustige Blätter–*Stalin as Snow White: "Mirror, mirror, tell me who am I . . ."*

▽ *From* La Razón *of Buenos Aires: the Russian bear awakes, much to Hitler's consternation. But the Führer managed to send it to sleep again with the November talks.*

△ *Cordiality all round as Molotov meets Göring, Hitler's trusted right hand. Seven months later, Göring's Luftwaffe would be using the benefits it had gained from the respite resulting from these talks to blast open the way for the Panzers.*

war which Moscow did not want in the present state of the conflict and, come to that, in the present state of the Soviet armed forces.

Hitler signs the "Barbarossa" directive

Every historian of this period of modern history has established a cause-effect relationship between the failure of these talks in Berlin and the signature which the Führer wrote at the foot of each of the nine copies of his Directive No. 21–"Barbarossa"–on December 18, 1940.

"The German armed forces must be prepared, even before the conclusion of the war against England, *to crush Soviet Russia in a rapid campaign*."

During this intended campaign, the task of keeping up activity against Great Britain would be the task of the German Navy principally. The Luftwaffe would aid the navy in blockade operations, while maintaining a solid defence against attacks by the R.A.F. on the industrial centres of the Reich and occupied Europe.

The army, leaving behind only such forces as were necessary for maintaining security in the occupied nations of the West, would launch an offensive against the bulk of the Soviet forces deployed in western Russia. These Russian forces were to be dislocated by savage armoured thrusts, which were to push on right into Russia and thus prevent Soviet forces from falling back into their vast rear areas. The final objective for Operation "Barbarossa" was fixed as the line Astrakhan'–the Volga–Gor'ky–Kotlas–Archangel.

The Luftwaffe's task

The Luftwaffe was to take part in the campaign with the main weight of its effective force utilised thus:

1. To protect German concentrations and industries in the east of the Reich from attacks by enemy aircraft;
2. To ensure support for the army at its main points of attack; and
3. At the end of the offensive to put out of action the industrial installations of the Urals area.

First three objectives: Kiev, Smolensk, Leningrad

The Führer envisaged three army groups, in two major concentrations, carrying out this gigantic operation:

1. South of the Pripet Marshes, which were to divide the western Russian theatre between the two major subunits, Army Group "A" (Rundstedt) was to concentrate around Lublin and drive rapidly on Kiev and along the right bank of the Dniepr; and
2. North of the Pripet Marshes and up to the Baltic:

a. The strongly equipped Army Group "B" (Bock) was to concentrate around Warsaw and take the area between the Dniepr and the Dvina, as far as Smolensk and Vitebsk; and
b. The more lightly equipped Army Group "C" (Leeb) was to thrust out from East Prussia through Lithuania and Latvia in the direction of Leningrad.

And then Moscow . . .

Hitler then planned that, once it had taken Smolensk, Army Group "B" would turn from Moscow and advance towards Leningrad in support of Army Group "C". The fall of Kronstadt, which would follow upon that of Leningrad, would wipe out Russian naval forces in the Baltic. Then the two army groups would turn on Moscow together.

. . . and Murmansk

In this operation Hitler could count on the armed support of Rumania and Finland. With the latter's help a German detachment from Norway would seize Murmansk.

Master of the only Arctic port usable all the year round, he would be able to sever the most convenient link between the U.S.S.R., Great Britain, and the U.S.

The map exercises and studies carried out as a result of Hitler's decision of July 31 caused misgivings about the whole idea of the operation in the minds of certain members of the German High Command, notably Field-Marshal von Brauchitsch and especially Colonel-General Halder. They thought that as soon as the German forces had cleared the Dniepr-Dvina corridor, where the rivers run parallel to each other, the objective of Army Group "B" should be not Leningrad but Moscow. In this they were not looking for a mere prestige victory, but reckoned that the fall of Moscow would deprive the Russians of their administrative centre and important industrial resources. They were also influenced by the fact that Moscow was the centre of most of the lines of communication. Once the Germans had reached the other side of Moscow, the Russians would be left with no strategic mainline railway running north-south. The capture of Moscow would therefore also deprive the Soviet High Command of any possibility of large-scale manoeuvre.

Moreover, Brauchitsch, Halder, and Paulus thought that to score an initial victory on the Moscow front would have such an impact that the Russians would do everything in their power to stop any German advance in this direction. They would thus be forced to fight a delaying battle between Smolensk and their capital. Here the last organised forces of the Soviet Union would be engaged, attacked, out-manoeuvred, broken up, and wiped out in accordance with the strictest doctrine of Clausewitz and his school.

The last argument in favour of this direct attack on Moscow was that it would save time. By cutting out the flanking attack on Leningrad it was more likely that the tight schedule of "Barbarossa" could be adhered to. The Führer's directive had said that, once launched on May 15, the operation had to be concluded by October 15. There was all the more reason to make haste, as when the High Command had asked Hitler to lay in stocks of special equipment for a winter campaign he had refused, saying that industrial production was not to be overloaded and he had to avoid severe restrictions on the German people.

Field-Marshal von Brauchitsch and his chief-of-staff do not appear to have discussed their objections frankly with Hitler, not only from the fear of his sarcasm but also because they thought that the matter was not urgent, an opinion based on Moltke's statement that no plan of

▽ Preparations for the war in the East: German armour begins the long journey from France to its jump-off points in Poland.

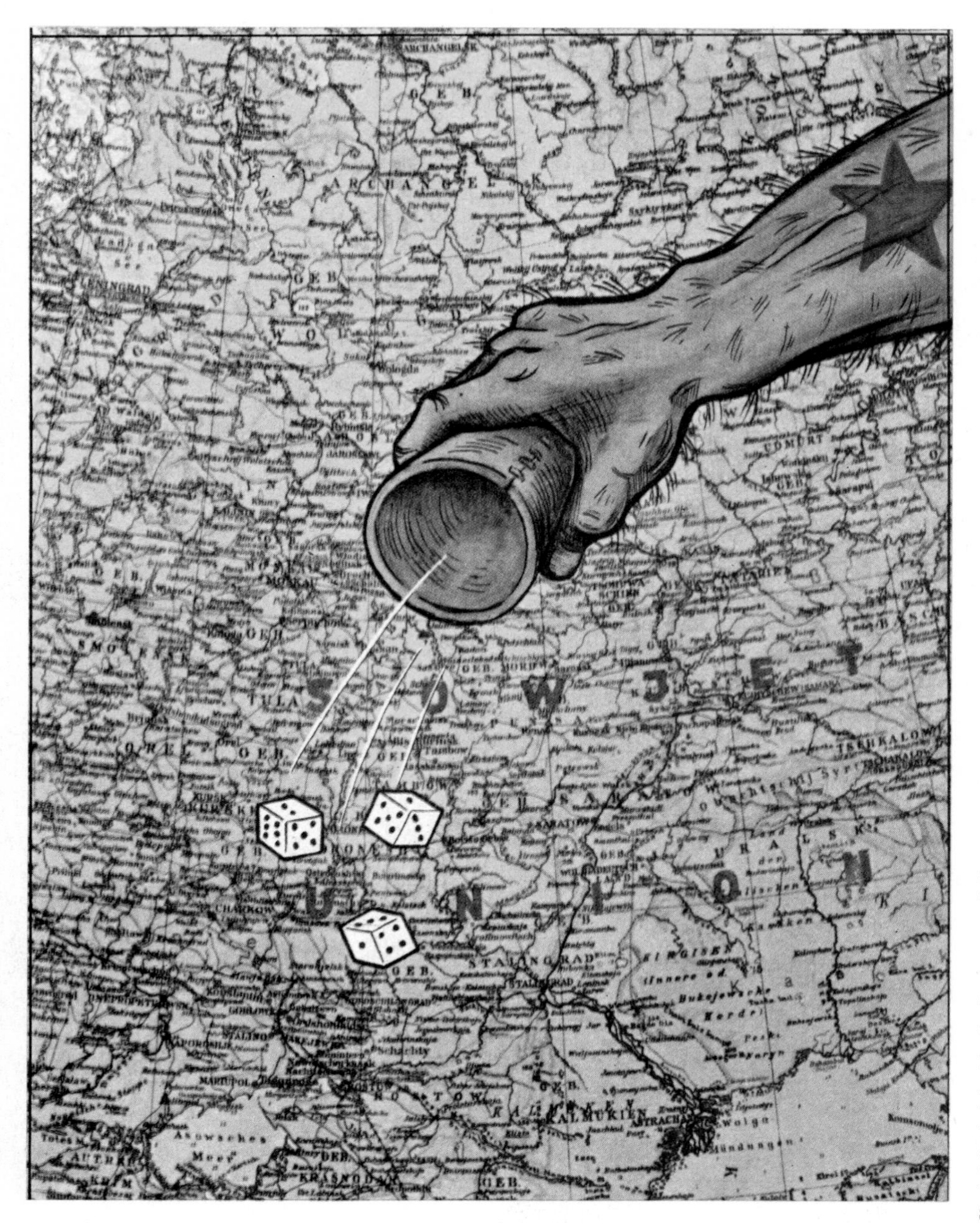

▵ *"The die is cast", announces the* Lustige Blätter. *So it was, but Germany's latest throw was to bring her "Thousand-Year Reich" tumbling down in less than four years after the invasion of the Soviet Union.*

operations can be expected to provide any reliable forecast beyond the first engagement with the enemy's main forces. For the moment they had to succeed in their allotted task of concentration and then secure a resounding initial victory both in the Ukraine and in Belorussia. After this they would have time to think out how to exploit their victory and persuade the High Command to agree to a direct thrust towards Moscow.

They did not take into account Hitler and his obstinacy, though this was well known.

Logistic preparations

Meanwhile a vast organisation programme was afoot in the German High Command. Fifty large new units had to be created and 3,400,000 men, 600,000 vehicles, and 600,000 horses transported and concentrated between the Black Sea and the Baltic, their on-the-spot feeding had to be arranged, and stocks of supplies sufficient to allow them to push forward at the required speed in a country with poor communications had to be amassed. And all this had to be done without prejudicing such demands as might arise from other theatres of war and without arousing any suspicions on the other side.

The concentration of these enormous quantities of men and material required the movement of 17,000 trains. To ensure secrecy this was staggered between early March and June 22, 1941.

By the end of February there were 25 divisions in the concentration area; seven more arrived in March, 13 in April, 30 in May, and 51 between June 1 and 22. These 126 divisions were increased by a further 19 from the High Command reserves which were moved up into battle after the outbreak of hostilities. At the same time the Luftwaffe, leaving 1,500 planes for operations against England, concentrated some 2,000 first-line aircraft to support "Barbarossa": 720 fighters, 1,160 high altitude and dive-bombers, and 120 tactical and strategic reconnaissance planes, all of which required, in Poland alone, the establishment or rebuilding of 250 airfields. To relieve O.K.H., which was to act as Operational G.H.Q. on the Eastern Front, Hitler gave O.K.W. authority over all the other theatres of war, including North Finland, where four German divisions were to force their way through the tundra towards Murmansk and the White Sea. The other theatres were held by 55 divisions, allocated as follows:

Norway and Denmark:	8
France, Belgium, and Holland:	38
The Balkans:	7
Libya:	2

Was this an "annoying frittering away of resources" as Colonel-General Guderian says in his book *Panzer Leader*? He would seem to be exaggerating, as out of these 55 divisions, 32 were so short of men and material as to be considered for the moment unfit for use at the front. Of the 21 armoured divisions, only the 15th and the 21st Panzer Divisions, allotted to the *Afrika Korps*, did not take part in the Eastern offensive. These two divisions had less than 300 tanks between them, whereas Kleist, Guderian, Hoth, and Hoeppner had exactly 3,332 on June 22, 1941.

△ *More top-level discussions between Mussolini and his generals and the German High Command–this time on the subject of Italy's participation in the coming invasion of Soviet Russia. Hitler did not ask for Italian aid, but the Duce, as always, refused point-blank to be eclipsed by his German colleague.*

CHAPTER 38
Diplomatic Prelude

Between Molotov's return to Moscow and dawn on June 22, Soviet policy described a curve, the summit of which was the signing of the Soviet-Yugoslav Treaty of Friendship during the night of April 5–6 in the Kremlin. This curve followed faithfully the vicissitudes of Axis strategy. It will be recalled that Hitler signed his "Marita" directive on December 13, 1940, committing him to a diversion in the Balkans. This he would willingly have avoided as it caused him to cross Bulgarian territory, which the Soviet Union considered as one of its preserves. So, when he renewed the Soviet-German agreements on supplies, Molotov, at the first rumour that the Germans were preparing to cross the Danube, sent through *Tass* a very clear warning to the German Government.

The day after Bulgaria joined the Tripartite Pact, Molotov was not satisfied with the soothing explanations which the German Ambassador had been instructed, by the orders of the Wilhelmstrasse, to offer to him. On the basis of his communiqué of November 26 he pointed out that Moscow considered Bulgarian territory as coming within the Soviet security zone and that Berlin was well aware of this; that was why, his memorandum to Schulenburg concluded, "the German Government must realise that it cannot count on

the support of the Soviet Union for its actions in Bulgaria."

As this memorandum contained no threat of reprisals, Hitler could afford to ignore it. King Boris's Minister in Moscow, Altinov, was severely reprimanded, and the reprimand was made public, while Molotov's remarks to the German Ambassador were not. On March 4 a communiqué from the People's Commissar for Foreign Affairs, and not a *Tass* despatch, stated that Altinov had received the following reply from Vice-Commissar Vishinsky: "The Soviet Government cannot agree with the Bulgarian Government that the latter's decision was correct, since this decision, whatever the desires of the Bulgarian Government, will help to spread and not to reduce the area of war and draw Bulgaria into the conflict. The Soviet Government, faithful to its policy of peace, cannot support the Bulgarian Government in its new policy."

A stinging rebuke, indeed, but one which carried no threat of action, or even suggestion of a threat.

Moscow encourages Ankara to resist . . .

The presence of the Wehrmacht on Bulgarian soil nevertheless led Moscow to encourage Turkey to resist. Statements were exchanged and published to this effect on March 25. Far from associating herself with an aggressor who would force the Turks to take up arms to defend their territory, the U.S.S.R., sticking to a Russo-Turkish non-aggression pact still in force, assured Turkey of her neutrality and her complete understanding, and the Ankara Government undertook similar promises in the event of the Soviet Union herself being attacked.

. . . and signs a treaty of friendship with Belgrade

The Yugoslav Government which came to power after the coup d'état of March 27 decided to resume the friendly relations with Russia which had existed between Belgrade and St. Petersburg from 1903 to 1917. After some hesitation Stalin and Molotov replied, accepting the overtures brought to them by Peter II's Minister in Moscow, Milan Gabrilovic. And so, on the morning of April 6 the world learnt simultaneously of the signing of a Pact of Non-Aggression and Friendship between the two states and of the savage aerial attack on Belgrade, the first stage of the German onslaught.

The Soviet Government's only reaction to this latter event was a sharp reprimand from Vishinsky to the Hungarian Minister who, on April 13, had come to inform him that his country, notwithstanding its recently-signed non-aggression pact with Belgrade, supported the German action and would make no official recrimination. Even better, on the same day, when the Soviet authorities were seeing off the Japanese Minister, Yosuke Matsuoka, who had just signed a non-aggression pact with Molotov, Stalin made it abundantly clear that he had changed his position. The curious scene was recorded by Grigore Gafencu:

"When the Japanese Minister, surrounded by members of his mission, finally arrived at the station where diplomats, economists, and military attachés from the Axis powers were waiting for him, a second dramatic event occured. In the general commotion of astonished onlookers, bustling policemen and soldiers running up at the double, Stalin appeared at the top of the steps and walked forward to meet the Japanese. His appearance caused utter astonishment among the diplomats: the Russian ruler, whose public appearances were so rare, had never paid such an honour to a visiting guest. However, Stalin walked uncertainly, as though light-headed from the open air, contact with the people, and his own audacity. As if each onlooker were a brother, he shook the hands of travellers and employees standing around on the platform. Then, after greeting his Japanese guest, who stepped forward gravely to meet him, looking solemn and moved, he turned to the medal-bedecked group of military attachés and saluted all the officers who were presented to him. He stopped in front of Colonel Krebs of the German General Staff, standing stiffly at attention, put his arm round his neck and winked at him, saying 'We shall always be friends, eh?'"

A fortnight previously the tiny Japanese Minister had had another opportunity of appreciating his own popularity when he had stayed in Berlin for important talks with Hitler and Ribbentrop.

"The clear-sounding name of this little statesman, who came on an official visit to Germany at the end of March 1941, was on every Berliner's lips. It so happened that they were able to pronounce it clearly, without distorting it . . . I often had the occasion to go out with Matsuoka in an open car through the streets of the city and I was able to see the reaction of the people at first hand. 'It's Matsuoka,' the crowds would say as they gathered either in front of the Chancellery or before the Bellevue Palace in the Tiergarten. 'Take care the little man doesn't fall under the car,' a fat Berliner shouted to me one day from among the crowd of spectators. Matsuoka thought the crowd was giving him an ovation and he raised his top hat with truly oriental solemnity."

Perhaps it was in order to appease the once again victorious Hitler, or at least to gain time, that Joseph Stalin, then Secretary of the Communist Party of the U.S.S.R., became Chairman of the Council of People's Commissars on May 7, 1941.

◁ German troops cross into Bulgaria during the build-up on the southern flank. The massing of Wehrmacht forces in Bulgaria was one of the most obvious indications of Hitler's future intentions in eastern Europe.
◁▽ Field-Marshal List, the German commander in Bulgaria, in discussion with King Boris.
▽ Wehrmacht transports pour across the Danube into Bulgaria over an enormous, dual-carriageway pontoon bridge.

Die Gefahr des
Bolschewismus

In this he replaced the intractable Molotov who, however, retained the Ministry of Foreign Affairs. This was the version Schulenburg gave the Wilhelmstrasse and it was very likely the right one. Anyhow, on the following day the Ministers of Belgium, Norway, and even the unfortunate Gabrilovic were ignominiously expelled from Soviet territory.

As quickly as possible Stalin attempted to get back to the spirit of the Soviet-German Pact of August 23, 1939 and hoped to succeed in appeasing Hitler. Amid the rumours of war circulating from the Atlantic to the Urals, on June 14 he dictated to the official *Tass* Agency the following communiqué which, after implicating the person of Sir Stafford Cripps, the British Ambassador to Moscow, brought everything back to its essentials and intensified Russian advances to the Third Reich:

"According to these rumours," *Tass* said:

"1. Germany has made economic and territorial demands on the U.S.S.R. and these are at present the subject of negotiations between Germany and the U.S.S.R. for the conclusion of a new and closer agreement;
2. The U.S.S.R. has rejected these demands and as a result Germany has begun to concentrate her troops on the frontier of the U.S.S.R. in order to attack the Soviet Union; and
3. The Soviet Union on its side has begun intensive preparations for war against Germany and has concentrated her troops along the German border.

"In spite of the evident absurdity of these rumours, responsible circles in Moscow have thought it necessary – because of the persistence of such false reports – to authorise *Tass* to state that the rumours are the clumsy product of a propaganda campaign by the enemies of the U.S.S.R. and Germany and who are interested in spreading the war. *Tass* states that:

"1. Germany has made no claims of any kind and does not propose any closer agreement with the Soviet Union; for these reasons negotiations on this matter cannot have taken place;
2. According to Soviet information Germany is respecting the Soviet-German Non-Aggression Pact as scrupulously as is the Soviet Union. This is why Soviet circles consider that rumours to the effect that Germany is contemplating breaking this pact and attacking the Soviet Union are without any foundation. Recent movements of German troops liberated from the Balkan campaign to regions east and north-east of Germany have other purposes and do not affect Soviet-German relations;
3. In accordance with its policy of peace the Soviet Union has respected and intends to respect the conditions of the Soviet-German Non-Aggression Pact. Rumours that the Soviet Union is preparing for war against Germany are untrue and provocative; and
4. The summer mobilisation of the Red Army reservists and the manoeuvres which will follow continuously are intended merely for the training of the troops and the inspection of the running of the railways, as is done every year. To claim that these current measures by the Red Army are directed against Germany is, to say the least, absurd."

As usual the Soviet press echoed this communiqué and directed its bitterest attacks at Perfidious Albion's plutocratic warmongers, who fancied they could bring the two nations into conflict.

This explains Molotov's question to the German Ambassador at dawn on June 22, 1941. Schulenburg had come to inform him that, by reason of the insupportable pressure along the demarcation line of Russian troops on the Germans, the latter had been given the order to enter Soviet territory. Molotov replied: "It is war. Your planes have just bombed some ten open towns. Do you think we deserved that?"

History's answer must be "no". Everything goes to show that at this precise moment Communist Russia was earnestly searching for terms of a new and fruitful agreement with Nazi Germany.

At the same moment the Foreign Office sent the news to Chequers, where Churchill was peacefully asleep. This dramatic event is one more illustration of British phlegm, as the Prime Minister's private secretary's account shows:

"I was awoken at 4 a.m. the following morning by a telephone message from the F.O. to the effect that Germany had attacked Russia. The P.M. had always said that he was never to be woken up for anything but Invasion (of England). I therefore postponed telling him till 8 a.m. His only comment was, 'Tell the B.B.C. I will broadcast at 9 to-night.' He began to prepare the speech at 11 a.m., and devoted the whole day to it. . . . The speech was only ready at twenty minutes to nine."

△ *They turned to Moscow for aid against German pressure, but did not save their country from Axis subjugation: King Peter II of Yugoslavia and the former Regent, Prince Paul* (right).
◁ *Since 1918, Germany's traditional bogeyman image of Soviet Russia: the spectre of Bolshevism. Hitler's announcement to his troops on the eve of Barbarossa had it pat: Russia must be destroyed "in order to save the whole of European civilisation and culture."*

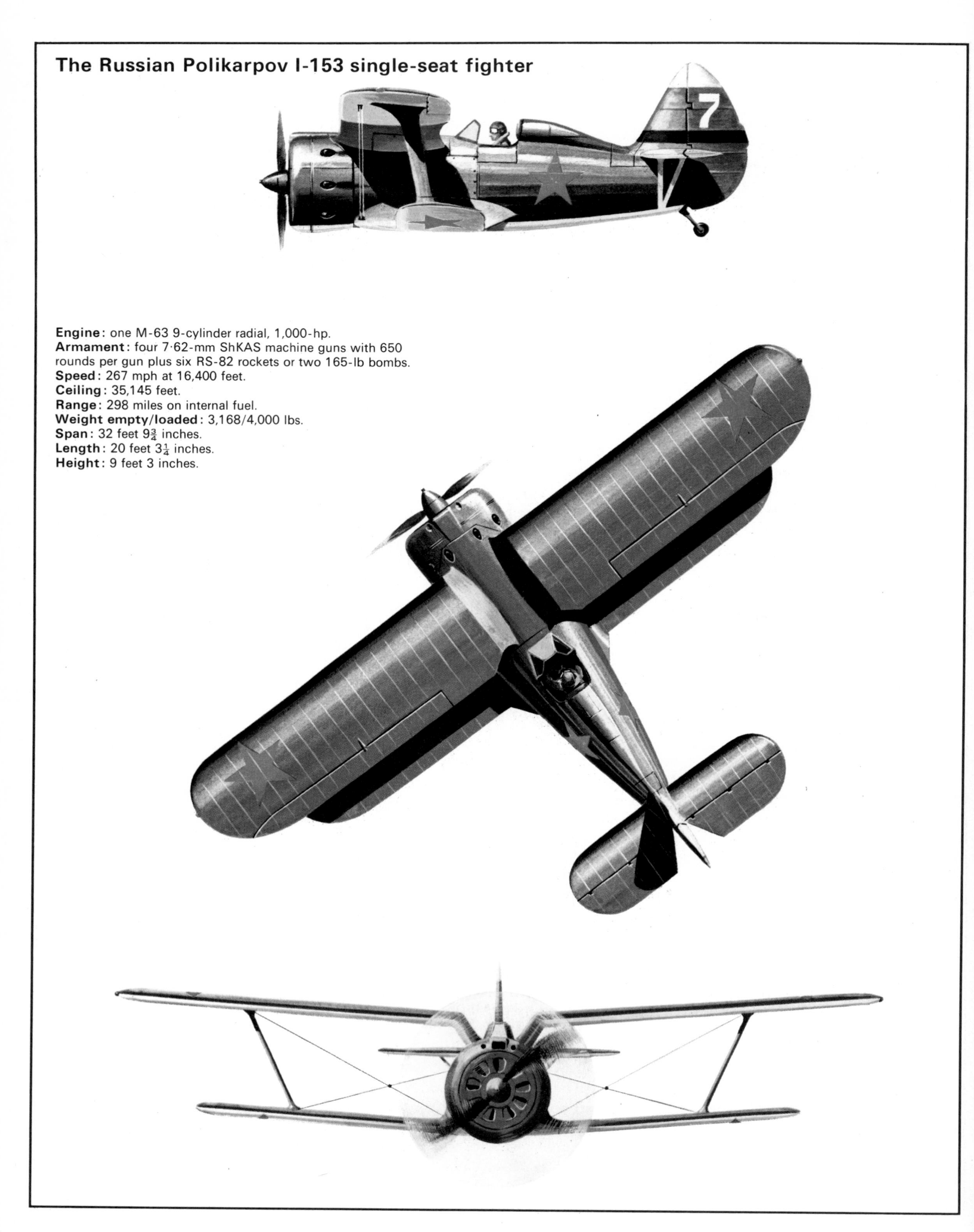

The Russian Polikarpov I-153 single-seat fighter

Engine: one M-63 9-cylinder radial, 1,000-hp.
Armament: four 7·62-mm ShKAS machine guns with 650 rounds per gun plus six RS-82 rockets or two 165-lb bombs.
Speed: 267 mph at 16,400 feet.
Ceiling: 35,145 feet.
Range: 298 miles on internal fuel.
Weight empty/loaded: 3,168/4,000 lbs.
Span: 32 feet $9\frac{3}{4}$ inches.
Length: 20 feet $3\frac{1}{4}$ inches.
Height: 9 feet 3 inches.

The German Henschel 123A single-seat ground attack aircraft

Engine: one B.M.W. 132D 9-cylinder radial, 870-hp.
Armament: two 7·92-mm MG 17 machine guns and one 550-lb or four 110-lb bombs.
Speed: 214 mph at 4,000 feet.
Ceiling: 29,530 feet.
Range: 530 miles.
Weight empty/loaded: 3,080/4,652 lbs.
Span: 34 feet $5\frac{1}{3}$ inches.
Length: 27 feet 4 inches.
Height: 10 feet $6\frac{1}{3}$ inches.

Though there can be little doubt that Germany's initial victories against Russia were the result of surprise, superior training at all levels, and better strategic and tactical planning, as well as the intelligent way in which she capitalised on the advantages of her *matériel*, it should not be thought that Russian weapons were completely outclassed by those of the Germans. In armour and artillery, for example, the Russians led the world, though their technological superiority in such weapons was thrown away by poor strategic and tactical planning.

In the field of military aviation, Russia had been in the forefront of the development of the heavy bomber, cannon and missiles for use in fighters and ground attack aircraft, and the modern monoplane fighter, with a retractable undercarriage and low wing configuration. But the opposing school of thought, which placed the fighter's manoeuvrability above speed, was still strong in Russia, and both monoplane and biplane fighters appeared in the middle 1930's.

We have already seen the former, the "*Ishak*", on page 146. The best of the latter type was the Polikarpov I-153 "*Chaika*" (Gull), which appears on page 510. This was a development of the same designer's earlier I-15 biplane fighter of 1933, from which it differed principally in being fitted with a retractable undercarriage. The "*Chaika*" (the name clearly derived from the gull-wing aspect of the upper wing) first appeared in 1935, and was an immediate success.

Flown operationally in the Spanish Civil War and in the "border incidents" against Japan in 1938, the success of the I-153 seemed to confirm the value of the fast but extremely agile biplane against the early monoplanes, especially when the latter had fixed undercarriages, as did the Japanese Ki-27. The type was used extensively in the "Winter War", great numbers having been built after the successes in Mongolia, but it was definitely outclassed by the Messerschmitt Bf 109 in 1941. Its one saving grace was that its manoeuvrability enabled competent pilots to escape destruction, even if they could not shoot down the invaders' aircraft.

The biplane was not limited to the Russian side in 1941, however, as the Germans also employed such a type, though it was a ground attack aircraft, not a fighter. This was the Henschel Hs 123A, which appears on page 511. This neat biplane was flown for the first time on May 8, 1935 by Ernst Udet, who was primarily responsible for the adoption of the dive-bomber by the Luftwaffe. After a small batch of pre-production machines had been built in 1936, the first and only production series, the Hs 123A-1, entered service in the early months of 1937. A few were sent to Spain for combat testing.

The type was obsolete by 1939, but achieved notable successes in Poland, France, and Russia after effective fighter opposition had been removed. It was the Luftwaffe's last operational biplane, and soldiered on to the end of the war in secondary tasks such as supply dropping and target towing.

Germany's best fighter in June 1941 was the Messerschmitt Bf 109F (p. 513). This model had replaced the 109E on the production lines late in 1940, the first examples reaching front line units in January 1941. The 109F had the same basic structure as the E, but aerodynamically it had been considerably cleaned up. Note the smoother contours of the nose, the larger and more rounded spinner, the shallower underwing radiators, the redesigned supercharger air intake (on the left hand side of the fuselage, above the wing leading edge), to make better use of ram effect, the more rounded wingtips and rudder, the absence of tailplane bracing struts, and the retractable tail wheel. These refinements, combined with the more powerful DB 601 engine, made the 109F the best aircraft of the series. For though later models were faster and better armed, they lost much of the delicacy of control in the process.

The 109F did not, however, enter service without problems: at first the tailplane spar was prone to breakage, but the trouble was traced to vibration and cured. There was also considerable dissatisfaction with the armament, which had been lightened compared with the 109E. Later models had a 20-mm cannon in the nose instead of the 15-mm one.

The aircraft illustrated is in the II *Gruppe* markings of the *Geschwader* adjutant of *Jagdgeschwader* 54 "*Grünherz*".

In armour the Russians had a definite qualitative, as well as quantitative, advantage over the Germans, and it was lucky indeed for the latter that they attacked Russia before she had had time to complete the reorganisation of her armoured forces. Though the German would probably still have succeeded in pushing deep into Russia, they would have found the going much harder.

Illustrated on page 521 is the T-35B, one of Russia's main tanks in the 1930's, but which was being phased out at the time of the German attack. The T-35's still in service were used in the infantry support rôle.

The type had been inspired by the British Independent and the French *Char de Rupture* 2C and appeared in 1932. It was intended to operate independently, which accounts for the multiplicity and all-round disposition of its armament – an anti-tank gun in the central turret, and smaller guns and machine guns in the subsidiary turrets, for use against entrenched positions and infantry.

The T-35A had improved 45-mm guns and appeared in 1935, and the T-35B, with 50-mm instead of 30-mm armour, the year after that.

The best Russian tank, together with the T-34, was the KV-1, which was named after Klimenti Voroshilov, Marshal of the Soviet Union and Deputy Premier. This tank appears on page 524.

The main failing of tanks such as the T-35 was the number of turrets, which made control in battle difficult. Such a multiplicity of turrets was the penalty paid for not having a gun that could fire both high explosive and armour piercing shell, the one being useful only against infantry and fortified positions and the other against tanks. But by 1938 the Russians had developed a gun that could fire both high explosive (H.E.) and armour piercing (A.P.) shell.

The result was the KV-1, which was designed by a team under I.S. Kotin. The prototype appeared in 1939 and gave every indication that the production version would be an excellent tank. The KV-1 had the same main armament as the T-34, and an uprated development of the latter's engine, thus obviating the problems so often encountered in the design of these important components, but was otherwise completely different from the T-34. It was armoured on a heavier basis, although the armour was not as well sloped or as smooth as that on the T-34. Nevertheless, this was proof against the German 3.7-cm anti-tank gun, and when the 5-cm gun began to appear in significant numbers, extra armour was bolted to the sides of the next model, the KV-1B. The last model, the KV-1C, also appeared in 1941, and differed principally from its forerunners in having a cast turret in place of the earlier fabricated turret.

One final feature of the KV-1 is particularly noteworthy – the use of unarmoured and jettisonable fuel tanks (two on each side of the hull abreast of the turret) for its less flammable diesel oil.

The German Messerschmitt Bf 109F single-seat fighter

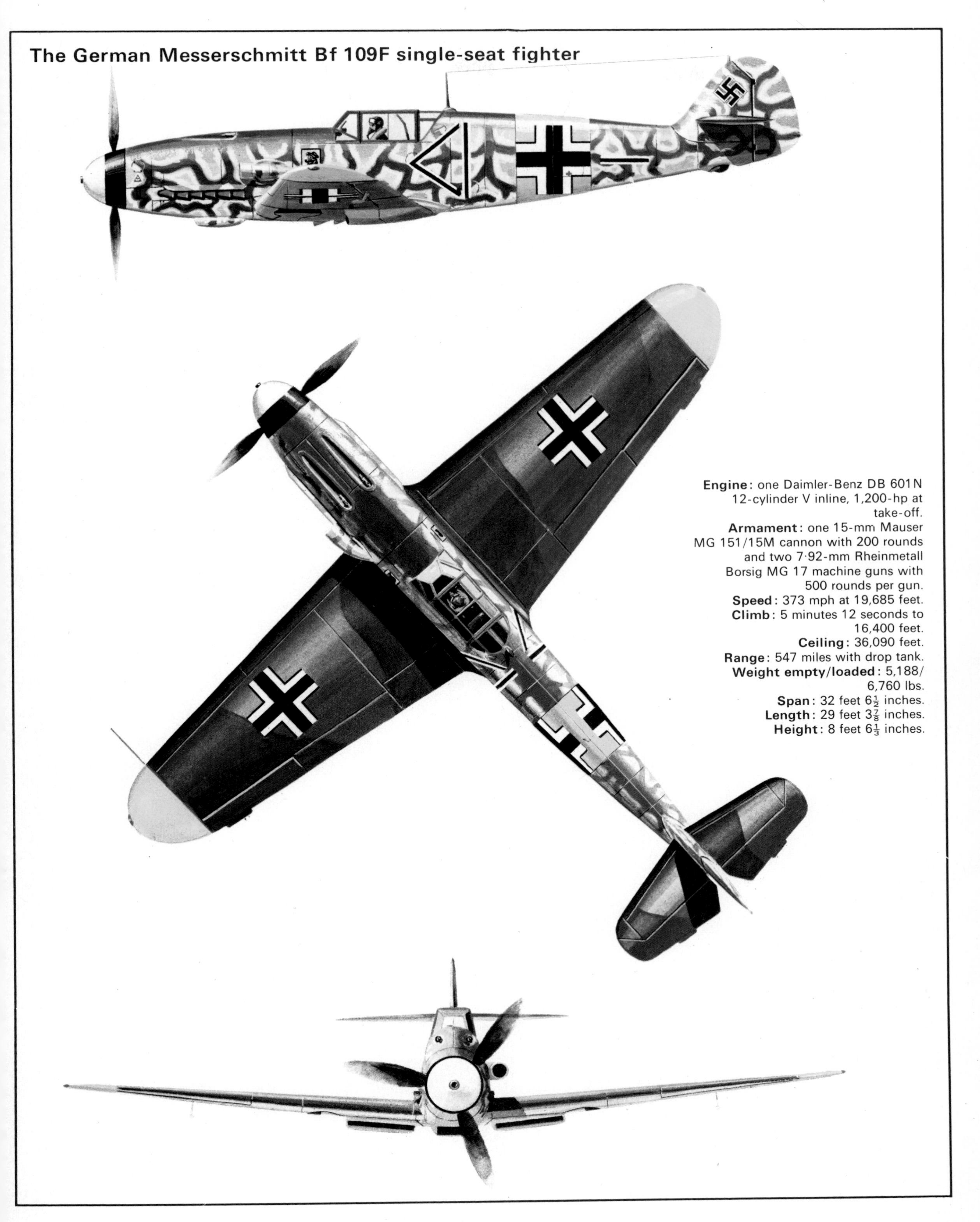

Engine: one Daimler-Benz DB 601N 12-cylinder V inline, 1,200-hp at take-off.
Armament: one 15-mm Mauser MG 151/15M cannon with 200 rounds and two 7·92-mm Rheinmetall Borsig MG 17 machine guns with 500 rounds per gun.
Speed: 373 mph at 19,685 feet.
Climb: 5 minutes 12 seconds to 16,400 feet.
Ceiling: 36,090 feet.
Range: 547 miles with drop tank.
Weight empty/loaded: 5,188/6,760 lbs.
Span: 32 feet $6\frac{1}{2}$ inches.
Length: 29 feet $3\frac{7}{8}$ inches.
Height: 8 feet $6\frac{1}{3}$ inches.

CHAPTER 39

The Armies Face to Face

On June 22, 1941, at dawn, 3,400,000 Germans launched a surprise attack on the Soviet Union, defended by the 4,700,000 men of the Red Army, as Russia's army was called. In the numbers engaged and the losses suffered on both sides, this titanic struggle, unprecedented in human history, had no equal in any other theatre of operations in World War II. It would go on until the annihilation of the Wehrmacht, expressed in the smoking ruins of Berlin, and the signing of the instrument of unconditional surrender by Field-Marshal Keitel, followed by Grand-Admiral von Friedeburg and Colonel-General Stumpff of the Luftwaffe, in the presence of Marshal of the U.S.S.R. Georgi Zhukov, General Carl Spaatz of the United States Army Air Force, Air Chief-Marshal Sir Arthur Tedder of the R.A.F., and General de Lattre de Tassigny of France.

It must be stated in introduction that there are many aspects of this tragic struggle which, even today, have not been clarified. There is an abundant German bibliography on the Eastern Front operations, in the form of memoirs, general or specialised histories, monographs and published documents, but nothing of the kind is available on the other side of the Iron Curtain. Historical research, which suffered under Stalin, was also weak in the period of "destalinisation", and the disgrace of Nikita Kruschev was reflected in new instructions as imperious as those of previous epochs.

But does the quality of Soviet historical publication compensate for its lack of quantity? Not in the opinion of Alexander Werth, who was the *Sunday Times* correspondent in Moscow throughout the war. In the introduction to his book *Russia at War* he writes:

". . . but even the longest of them, the vast six-volume Russian *History of the Great Patriotic War of the Soviet Union* running to over two million words, and trying to cover not only the military operations, but 'everything', is singularly unsatisfactory in many ways. It contains an immense amount of valuable information which was not available under Stalin; but it is overburdened with names of persons, regiments and divisions and an endless variety of military and economic details. It is full of ever-recurring 'heroic' clichés."

Whatever their differences, all the Soviet authors consulted in German translation are in agreement on one point, or rather one dogma, summarised neatly by Colonel-General P. A. Kurochkin in his conclusion to the collective work entitled *The Most Important Operations of the Great Patriotic War:*

"The colossal victory of the Soviet armed forces in the Great Patriotic War proves indisputably the progressive nature of Soviet military skill and its incontestable superiority over the military art of bourgeois armies."

This condemnation evidently includes not only the defeated in that merciless war, but also Russia's British and American allies. And as the statement is "indisputable", those who dare to question it prove, by doing so, their incurable ignorance or cynical bad faith. Such doubters are anathematised as "bourgeois falsifiers of history".

German armour

After the problem of Soviet sources, the armed forces of the two giants who clashed on June 22 must be analysed.

As has already been described, the decisive stroke had been allotted to the armour. It is essential, then, to consider briefly the growth of this arm between May 10, 1940 and June 22, 1941, with the aid of the following table:

	1940	1941
Panzergruppen	1	4
Panzer or motorised corps	5	11
Panzer divisions	10	21
Motorised divisions	7	14

The number of armoured divisions had thus risen from 17 to 35, but this is not all: as a result of their battle experience in 1939 and 1940, the Germans had ceased production of the Pzkw I and II light tanks and up-gunned most of their 965 Pzkw III medium tanks with 5-cm guns. This tank and the Pzkw 38(t) formed the backbone of the *Panzerwaffe* or Armoured Forces. The number of Pzkw IV heavy tanks

◁ *German troops advance into Russia. By June 1941, with an unbroken string of victories to its credit, the Wehrmacht was the most highly-trained and battle-seasoned fighting force in the world. But the vast distances to be covered in Soviet Russia raised many doubts as to the chances of success . . .*

▵ *The eternal trio at the head of the German Armed Forces High Command: Hitler, Keitel, and Jodl. In the summer of 1941 the Führer's moral ascendancy over the German armed forces was at its height. Openly contemptuous of the Soviet régime and the Red Army, he radiated complete confidence: "We have only to kick in the door and the whole rotten structure will come tumbling down." And his directives for the conduct of "Barbarossa" were faithfully translated into action by the professionals of the High Command.*

armed with the short 7.5-cm gun had been increased from 278 to 517.

The introduction of tracked cross-country vehicles should have allowed an infantry battalion and a pioneer company to be attached to each armoured division, but this stage had not been reached by all units on June 22. In the German Army there were also 250 self-propelled guns, and these were to give excellent service in infantry support and anti-tank operations.

These improvements should not, however, hide the fact that German war industry, under Göring, had not adapted itself properly to meet the huge effort needed to equip these formations. The year before, the ten Panzer divisions in the army had shared 35 battalions of tanks. To maintain 21 Panzer divisions at the same strength, it would have been necessary to equip another 40 or so battalions, but only 22 had in fact been formed, and six of these were not combat-ready. Because of this, the average strength of the Panzer divisions had dropped from 258 to 196 tanks during the period in question.

Thus even before going into action the number of tanks available had fallen to a dangerously low level. And during the campaign itself, a further toll was taken as the summer dust, autumn mud, and winter snows decimated the Panzer divisions' equipment. In these circumstances, it would have seemed sensible to bring under-strength units up to establishment before attempting to win a quick victory. But Hitler had other ideas, and the combat troops waited in vain for replacements as Hitler, back in Germany, constantly ordered the creation of new divisions, which were still untried and not available for service.

This great effort to increase armoured strength, combined with the insufficiency of German production, obliged the German High Command to make up its vehicle stocks with booty from Poland and France, requisitions from occupied countries, and deliveries under the terms of the Rethondes armistice. Both Hoth and Guderian concur, however, in saying that these French vehicles were too light and delicate to survive in the face of the Russian climate and Soviet roads. The situation soon became more serious as the problem of spare parts reared its ugly head.

The German infantry, including mountain troops, totalled 129 divisions at the end of the French campaign. By June 22, 1941, it had increased to 162 divisions made up into 47 corps. Luckily, the 27 corps which were to invade Russia on the 22nd had also been able to stock their motor pools with vehicles captured in 1939 and 1940. But as with the armoured forces, this was to cause serious trouble after several months of campaigning. Finally, the standard 3.7-cm infantry anti-tank gun was gradually being superseded by the newer 5-cm gun.

But Russia's strength of resistance lay not only with her regular armed forces. From information received by German Intelligence it was known that Moscow, if Russia were invaded, could also hurl the civil population of any areas overrun, organised into guerrilla units, against the flanks and communications of the invader. To combat this threat, O.K.H. formed nine Security Divisions (*Sicherungsdivisionen*) and allotted three to each army group. Though not capable of fighting regular troops in open country, they were nevertheless useful auxiliaries to front line troops, whom they relieved of the necessity of attending to their own security. The task of these divisions became more and more onerous as the Germans plunged deeper into Russian territory.

Germany's deployment

Including one cavalry division (1st Cavalry Division), which was removed from the front at the end of the year to be converted into an armoured division, the German Army could muster no less than 208 divisions in all theatres of war. Three-quarters of them, 153 to be exact, were engaged on the Eastern Front on June 22. Brauchitsch commanded 148 between the Black Sea and the Baltic deployed as follows:

1. *Right flank:* Army Group "South" (Rundstedt) with 42 divisions, including five Panzer and three motorised, divided between three armies and one *Panzergruppe*;
2. *Centre:* Army Group "Centre" (Bock), between Lublin and Suwałki, with 49 divisions, including nine Panzer, six motorised, and one cavalry, divided between two armies and two *Panzergruppen*; and
3. *Left flank:* Army Group "North" (Leeb) with 29 divisions, including three Panzer and two motorised, divided between two armies and one *Panzergruppe*.

In greater detail, these army groups broke down thus:

1. Army Group "South":
Moldavia: 11th Army (Colonel-General E. von Schobert); Carpathians–Lublin area: 17th Army (Colonel-General K. H. von Stülpnagel), *Panzergruppe* I (Colonel-General von Kleist) with 750 tanks, and 6th Army (Field-Marshal von Reichenau);
2. Army Group "Centre":
from south to north: *Panzergruppe* II (Colonel-General Guderian) with 930 tanks, 4th Army (Field-Marshal von Kluge), 9th Army (Colonel-General Strauss), and *Panzergruppe* III (Colonel-General Hoth) with 840 tanks; and
3. Army Group "North":
East Prussia: 16th Army (Colonel-General E. Busch), *Panzergruppe* IV Colonel-General Hoeppner) with 570 tanks, and 18th Army (Colonel-General G. von Küchler).

Thus the front line forces contained 120 divisions, including 17 of the 21 Panzer divisions (3,090 tanks), and 12 of the 14

△ *The Panzer spearheads of the German invasion, always probing ahead, by-passing pockets of resistance . . . .*
▽ *. . . and leaving the job of breaking up the Russian masses to the foot-slogging infantry, who trudged forwards in the dust of the Panzers.*

Δ *French recruiting poster for the* Waffen-S.S. *It was in Russia that* Waffen-S.S. *divisions were really blooded as fighting troops. Originally reserved for "Aryans", certified under the strictest conditions, the ranks of the* Waffen-S.S. *were soon thrown open to all nationalities in an attempt to meet the endless demand for manpower which was made by the Eastern Front. And the "United Europe" theme was the obvious cover-slogan and rallying-cry.*

motorised divisions. In reserve, O.K.H. had 2nd Army (Colonel-General von Weichs) with five corps made up of the 2nd and 5th Panzer Divisions, two motorised divisions, and no less than 24 infantry divisions.

In contrast, the German forces in Finland came under O.K.W. command and totalled five divisions or their equivalent.

In its struggle against the Soviet Union, the Third Reich could count on the help of Rumania, Hungary, and Slovakia, as well as the collaboration of Finland which, though she never signed any formal agreement with Germany, waged war at her side in order to recover the territory which she had lost to Russia by the terms of the treaty of March 12, 1940.

Marshal Antonescu put the Rumanian 3rd and 4th Armies at the service of his ally. These totalled 12 infantry divisions and her mountain, cavalry, and tank brigades, the equivalent of another two divisions. Admiral Horthy, the Regent of Hungary, played a more modest part, for Hungary had no bone to pick with Russia. Only one Hungarian corps, composed of a motorised brigade and two cavalry brigades, took part in the first phase of the campaign. Slovakia could not remain

Δ *Barbarossa propaganda: "The Crusade Against Bolshevism". Shown on the map are the national symbols for all the foreign contingents which fought beside the Wehrmacht in Russia. But their numbers were small in comparison with the German divisions deployed in Russia.*

neutral in such a conflict, and put a motorised brigade and two small infantry divisions under the command of Rundstedt, who also controlled the Hungarian and Rumanian contingents.

Between the Arctic Circle and the Gulf of Finland, Marshal Mannerheim took the field within 18 divisions, all eager for revenge after the Winter War.

It was not until the evening of June 21 that the Führer communicated his decision to invade Russia to his friend Mussolini in a long letter. Although Hitler made no request for aid, Mussolini proclaimed loudly that the dignity of Fascist Italy would not allow her to surrender her share in the "Crusade against Bolshevism". The *Corpo di spedizione italiano in Russia* (C.S.I.R.) was then formed under General Giovanni Messe with three infantry divisions: the partially motorised "Pasubio" and "Torino", and the "Celere". The corps formed part of the German 11th Army and went into battle on August 7, 1941.

At the news of the split between the allies of the Treaty of Moscow, General Franco authorised the recruitment of a Spanish infantry division, which was to repay the debt he had owed to Hitler since the Civil War. Composed of volunteers and named the *División Azul* (Blue Division), it went into line on the Novgorod front at the end of the summer of 1941 under General Muñoz Grande, who was later replaced by General Esteban Infantes.

Thus new satellites or associates had put about 50 divisions and brigades in the service of Germany. Nevertheless, with the exception of the Finnish Army, which did not belie its previous superb reputation, these allied forces were far less efficient than those of the Reich, in training, leadership, organisation, and equipment. Experience showed that three satellite units were required to complete a mission for which only two German units were necessary.

The Luftwaffe's part

The major ground offensive was also to be supported from the air, the four air fleets involved being allocated as follows:

1. *Luftflotte* IV (Colonel-General Alexander Löhr) to Army Group "South";
2. *Luftflotte* II (Field-Marshal Albert Kesselring) to Army Group "Centre";
3. *Luftflotte* I (Colonel-General Alfred Keller) to Army Group "North"; and
4. *Luftflotte* V (Colonel-General Hans-Jürgen Stumpff) to the mountain corps attacking Murmansk.

The Luftwaffe performed its tasks brilliantly. By the end of the first day of the invasion it had wiped out the Red Air Force as a fighting force for months to come, leaving the skies open for the Stukas to repeat the successes of Poland, France, the Balkans, and Crete against minimal opposition.

▽ German sappers repair a damaged bridge. The enormous length of the Wehrmacht's lines of communication demanded strenuous efforts of the rear area troops: bridge-building, road-making, and converting the Russian railway gauge to standard European gauge to keep supplies flowing to the front lines.

The Red Army

More than a quarter of a century after the unconditional surrender of the Third Reich, the initial deployment of the Soviet armed forces, as well as their structure and composition, are still much of a mystery. And since the secrecy which surrounds the subject has no relation, in view of the tremendous development of all arms, to present day security, the only conclusion that can be reached is that for reasons of domestic and international politics and propaganda, Moscow wishes to draw a veil over certain aspects of the great struggle.

The result is that, whereas with the aid of documents published in West Germany the German order of battle is known in detail down to divisional and even lower level, the semi-official *History of the Great Patriotic War* describes the Soviet forces, on the day of confrontation, only down to army level.

Between the Arctic and the Black Sea, the Red Army was deployed in five major groups:

1. Leningrad Military District (Rybachiy Peninsula to Vyborg, latterly Viipuri, some 750 miles), under Lieutenant-General M. M. Popov, was made up of:
   a. 14th Army (Lieutenant-General V. A. Frolov);
   b. 7th Army (Lieutenant-General F. D. Gorelenko); and
   c. 23rd Army (Lieutenant-General P. S. Pshennikov);
2. Baltic Special Military District (Polanga to the southern frontier of Lithuania, some 200 miles), under Colonel-General F. I. Kuznetsov, was made up of:
   a. 8th Army (Major-General P. P. Sobennikov); and
   b. 11th Army (Lieutenant-General V. I. Morosov);
3. West Special Military District (southern frontier of Lithuania to northern frontier of the Ukraine, some 280 miles), under General D. G. Pavlov, was made up of:
   a. 3rd Army (Lieutenant-General V. I.

The Russian T-35B heavy tank

Weight: 45 tons.
Crew: 10.
Armament: one 76.2-mm gun with 96 rounds, two 45-mm guns with 220 rounds, and five 7.62-mm machine guns with 10,000 rounds.
Armour: 50-mm maximum, 11-mm minimum.
Engine: one M-17 12-cylinder, 500-hp.
Speed: 18 mph.
Range: 93 miles.
Length: 32 feet 4 inches.
Width: 10 feet 8 inches.
Height: 11 feet 4 inches.

Once again the Luftwaffe's rôle would be to speed the advance of the ground forces, by commanding the sky over the battlefields of Russia and wreaking havoc in the Red Army's rear areas.

◁ *Göring talks with Werner Mölders, the first fighter pilot ever to score over 100 combat victories. As Göring's General of Fighters, Mölders showed considerable flair for administration. In June 1941 he was probably the most thoroughly respected leader the Luftwaffe had.*

△△ *Colonel-General Keller, commander of* Luftflotte *I, had the task of supporting Leeb's Army Group "North" during its drive on Leningrad.*

△ *Colonel-General Stumpff, commander of* Luftflotte *V. His charge was the far northern flank: based in Norway, it must strike at Russia's only sealane to Britain and do all in its power to assist the Finnish Army in its attacks.*

Kuznetsov);
b. 10th Army (Major-General K. D. Golubev); and
c. 4th Army (Major-General A. A. Korobkov);
4. Kiev Special Military District (northern frontier of the Ukraine to Lipkany, some 500 miles), under Colonel-General M. P. Kirponos, was made up of:
a. 5th Army (Major-General of Armoured Forces M. I. Potapov);
b. 6th Army (Lieutenant-General I. N. Muzychenko);
c. 26th Army (Lieutenant-General F. Ya. Kostenko); and
d. 12th Army (Major-General P. D. Ponedelin); and
5. Odessa Military District (Lipkany to the Black Sea, some 300 miles), under General I. V. Tyulenev, which shortly after the opening of hostilities divided its forces into:
a. 18th Army (Lieutenant-General A. K. Smirnov) and
b. 9th Army (Lieutenant-General Ya. T. Cherevichenko).

Although this list is not as full as one might desire, it does suggest an interesting conclusion: there are Major-Generals (brigade commanders) commanding armies, and Lieutenant-Generals (divisional commanders) at the head of Military Districts. Clearly the effects of Stalin's purge in the ranks of the Soviet High Command were still evident.

Its organisation has little worthy of comment about it except its somewhat meagre divisional anti-tank defences: 48 45-mm guns compared with 72 3·7-cm or 5-cm weapons in a German division.

Soviet armour

The constant changes made in her armoured forces go far to explain Russia's disasters in the first days of the campaign. The Red Army's first "mobile corps" had been formed in 1932, and the experience derived from it had been condensed into the *Provisional Field Regulations for the Direction and Use in Combat of Independent Mechanised Formations*. This was followed two years later by the *Provisional Instructions for Long-Range Combat*. Marshal Tukachevsky, who was responsible for these initiatives, was thus somewhat in advance of Colonel de Gaulle and the British tank theorists in getting concrete results.

Tukachevsky's liquidation in the purge together with the erroneous interpretation placed on the experience of the Spanish Civil War, put an end to these creative efforts. General D. G. Pavlov, who had been in Spain, was supported by Marshal K. Voroshilov in thinking it folly to send tanks into action independently of the infantry. Generals Shaposhnikov and Zhukov pleaded in vain for the independent mechanised corps, which was disbanded on Stalin's orders at the end of 1937.

"A serious error," writes the historian B. S. Telpukhovsky. But after the Polish and French campaigns, Stalin and his military advisers realised their mistake and set out to rectify the damage. They worked swiftly, and as early as July 1940 had finalised the organisation of the new mechanised corps. These were to include two armoured divisions (two tank regiments and one motorised rifle regiment) and one motorised division of exactly the reverse composition.

The *History of the Great Patriotic War* does not see it fit to reveal how many of these armoured divisions were operational on June 22. Although the total may be higher, it is possible to identify at least 11 mechanised corps by consulting other Russian sources. This would mean that there were 33 armoured and motorised divisions against the same number of German ones. Professor Hans-Adolf Jacobsen, a competent and scrupulous historian, raises the total of armoured and motorised divisions to 40. What is known for certain is that most of these formations were destroyed in the first few weeks of the campaign and could not be replaced, doubtless for lack of personnel. The armoured, mechanised, and motorised corps mentioned in 1942 were new formations, the result of amalgamating the remnants of the previous units and various independent brigades. It is not until the last phase of the war, from January 1945 onwards, that the Soviet order of battle contains armoured divisions in the Western sense of the term.

How good were Soviet tanks?

In a weapon as complicated as the tank, the importance of its equipment is more significant than in the infantry.

Marshal Klimenti Voroshilov, born in 1881, was People's Commissar for Defence during the Anglo-French negotiations for a Soviet alliance during the summer of 1939, in which he insisted that if the Red Army should go to Poland's aid it must be permitted to enter Polish territory. In the reshuffle of the Red Army after the bitter lessons of the Winter War against Finland, he became Deputy Premier and Chairman of the Defence Committee. On July 3, 1941, Stalin set up a State Defence Committee: himself, Voroshilov, Molotov, Beria, and Malenkov, and Voroshilov was given the job of defending Leningrad from the advance of Army Group "North". Stalin was forced to replace him with Zhukov, however, and remove Voroshilov from active command. Later in the war Voroshilov acted with much greater success as a military spokesman in discussions with the Allied leaders and commanders. His real talent lay in statesmanship and diplomacy rather than in military command. His stature in the Soviet High Command was considerable, however, and he gave his initials to the formidable "KV" heavy tank.

The Russian Klimenti Voroshilov (KV)-1A heavy tank

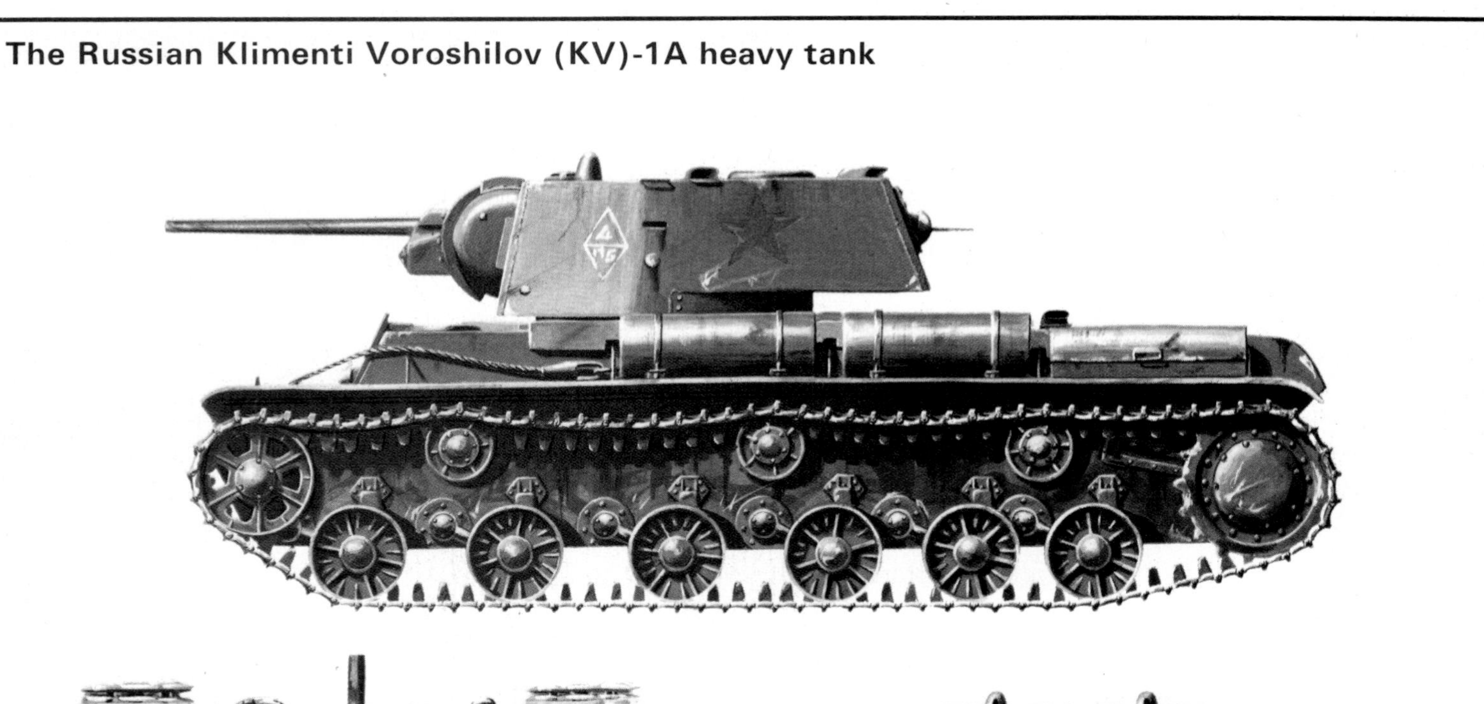

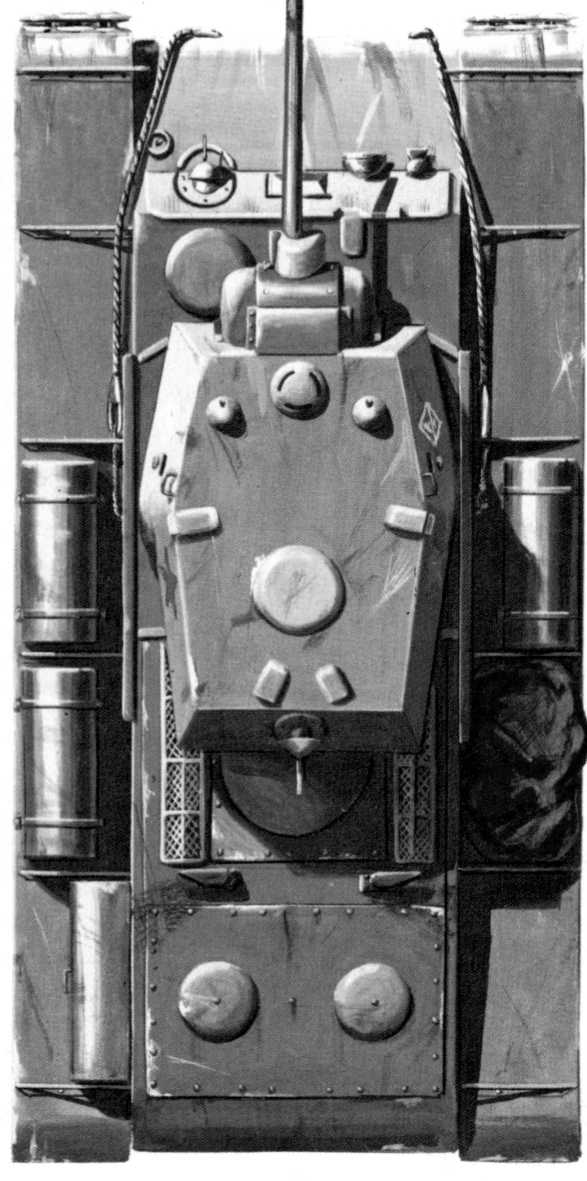

Weight: 43.5 tons.
Crew: 5.
Armament: one 76.2-mm F34 gun with 111 rounds and three 7.62-mm Degtyarev machine guns with 3,000 rounds.
Armour: glacis plate 75-mm; hull front 75-mm with a 31-mm plate added; hull sides 77-mm; decking 42-mm; belly 40-mm; turret front 82-mm; turret rear 92-mm; turret sides 100-mm; and mantlet 90-mm. (The armour figures are for the KV-1C, which differed from the KV-1A in having a cast turret almost identical in design with the KV-1A's fabricated turret, and thicker hull sides.)
Engine: one V-2K 12-cylinder diesel, 600-hp.
Speed: 21 mph.
Range: 210 miles.
Length: 22 feet 8 inches.
Width: 10 feet 11 inches.
Height: 9 feet 7 inches.

From this point of view, the numerous lessons learnt in the Spanish Civil War justify the belief that the Soviet T-26 and BT-7 light tanks, derived from original designs by Vickers of Great Britain and Christie of the United States, were superior to German machines of the same class and far better than Italian ones. On the other hand, they were greatly inferior to the medium and heavy tanks in service with the German Army.

The small number of T-35 and KV-2 heavy tanks, weighing 49 and 52 tons respectively, were to give the Germans some very unpleasant surprises in Lithuania and Galicia, but they were so clumsy that once the German infantry had got over their initial shock at the size of the tanks, they rapidly learned how to immobilise them with grenades before going in to attack them directly.

In contrast, M. I. Koshkin, A. A. Morozov, and N. A. Kucherenko had achieved in the T-34 the best combination of the three factors important in armour at the time: armament, armour, and mobility. The rate of fire of its 76.2-mm gun was superior to that of the 7.5-cm gun mounted by the heaviest German tank, the Pzkw IV, and its armour, in places 65-mm thick and well sloped, made it impervious to German anti-tank shells. Its mobility came from its 500-hp engine, wide tracks, and improved Christie-type suspension, and enabled it to tackle marshy or snow-covered ground in which its opponents bogged down.

At the same time as Soviet tacticians readopted Marshal Tukachevsky's theories, they kept the infantry tank, constructing the KV-1 for this purpose. Its speed was only 21 mph, compared with the 33 mph of the T-34, but this was not the disadvantage it might have been as the KV-1 was an infantry support weapon, and its lack of speed was compensated for by its massive hull, which gave it a weight of 43.5 tons, compared with the 26.3 tons of the T-34.

With 967 T-34's and 508 KV-1's, the Red Army had an enormous *matériel* superiority over the Germans who, on June 22, could put only 439 20-ton Pzkw IV's into the field. Yet this advantage was cancelled by several circumstances. Firstly, Stalin's blindness about Hitler's intentions had obliged the Soviet High Command to adopt unsuitable strategic plans. Secondly, Russian equipment was badly maintained: according to the *History of the Great Patriotic War*, only 29 per cent of the Russian tanks were ready to move out at a minute's notice because of the shortage of spare parts. Lastly, radio equipment was in extremely short supply and functioned only poorly.

△ *Guard of honour for General Gariboldi, inspecting troops of the Italian expeditionary force destined for service on the Eastern Front.*

Guderian's fears

The remarkable development of Soviet armour had escaped Hitler's eyes entirely, and had raised no more than unformulated doubts at O.K.H. But in his book *Panzer Leader*, General Guderian records the "curious incident" about Germany's possible enemy which led him to entertain doubts about the Third Reich's alleged invincibility:

"In the spring of 1941 Hitler had specifically ordered that a Russian military commission be shown over our tank schools and factories; in this order he had insisted that nothing be concealed from them. The Russian officers in question firmly refused to believe that the Panzer IV was in fact our heaviest tank. They said repeatedly that we must be hiding our newest models

△ *Heavy metal: German artillery in position on the Eastern Front. "Barbarossa" would be launched with a mammoth artillery barrage extending from the Black Sea to the Baltic at dawn on June 22, 1941 . . .*

from them, and complained that we were not carrying out Hitler's order to show them everything. The military commission was so insistent on this point that eventually our manufacturers and Ordnance Office officials concluded: 'It seems that the Russians must already possess better and heavier tanks than we do.' It was at the end of July, 1941, that the T-34 tank appeared at the front and the riddle of the new Russian model was solved."

The Red Air Force

Whatever the numerical superiority of the Red Air Force over the Luftwaffe, it merits only a brief mention in the calculation of Russian forces, since most of its few modern aircraft were surprised and destroyed on the ground in the first few hours of the campaign. In May 1941, Luftwaffe Intelligence estimated that the Red Air Force had 7,300 aircraft of all types, 4,000 of them first line, deployed in the west. It was later admitted that the figures were in error, greatly underestimating Soviet air strength.

Nevertheless, the Red Air Force would need at least a year to recover from the stunning blow inflicted on it by the Luftwaffe. In the interim, the Stukas of the Luftwaffe could attack Soviet armour and positions without hindrance, while the German A.A., now unemployed, could concentrate on anti-tank action, where its 8.8-cm guns achieved notable successes.

Soviet naval strength

We have already noted Stalin's desire to build up a strong navy in the chapter on German aid to Russia. But on June 22, 1941, the Soviet Navy possessed no fewer than 139 submarines, distributed thus: Arctic Ocean 14; the Baltic 74; and the Black Sea 51. In other classes of vessel the Russian Navy was weak, having only a few modern cruisers and destroyers, but this submarine fleet was the largest in the world.

Its size was not, however, matched by its successes. Between June 22, 1941 and May 8, 1945, it sank only 292,000 tons of shipping, compared with Germany's 14.5 million tons, the United States' 5.5 million tons, and Great Britain's 1.8 million tons. It is true that the Arctic, Baltic, and Black Sea offered far less in the way of prey than the North Atlantic, Pacific, and Mediterranean, but all the same, not until the end of 1944 were Soviet submarines able to interfere significantly with the seaborne supply or evacuation of German troops, and with imports of Swedish iron ore.

It must be admitted, however, that Germany's main lines of communication lay on land, and thus even had they been more efficient, there would have been little that they could do.

Airborne troops

The Soviet High Command had been the first in the world to recognise the value of airborne troops for operations in the enemy's rear, destroying his communications and cutting front line units off from their supplies and reinforcements. Under Tukachevsky's aegis, the first parachute units in the Red Army had been raised in 1935. But at the beginning of the Russian campaign such troops were hardly used, possibly because of the devastating losses suffered by the Red Air Force. Another reason is that after Tukachevsky's downfall Stalin and his military advisers had lost interest in the arm supported so ardently by their late victim, and its establishment and efficiency had declined.

△ Cavalry was also used by the Germans in Russia. The regular army's East Prussian cavalry division was earmarked for Army Group Centre; these men belong to one of the two Waffen-S.S. *cavalry regiments which were formed into a brigade in August 1941.*

Surprise on the side of the Germans

Such were the strengths and weakness of the Soviet land, sea, and air forces. But the defeats which the Russians suffered in four continuous months, and the German's advance to the suburbs of Moscow, cannot be explained without mentioning the factor of surprise, of which the invaders made full use right from the beginning of the campaign. In fact, Hitler and O.K.H. had camouflaged as best they could the 153 German divisions which would go into the

▷ *Help from the Spaniards: a colour-bearer of the "Blue Division" sent by Franco to fight on the Eastern Front under the command of General Muñoz-Grande.*

▽ "Schnell Heinz" *Guderian, the Panzer virtuoso. His initial reaction to the idea of invading Soviet Russia was unequivocal. "When they spread out a map of Russia before me I could scarcely believe my eyes . . . I made no attempt to conceal my disappointment and disgust . . . All the men of the O.K.W. and the O.K.H. with whom I spoke evinced an unshakable optimism and were quite impervious to criticism or objections."*

attack on June 22, and they had also made several diversionary feints.

"For two days," writes Paul Carell, "they had been lying in the dark pine-woods with their tanks and their vehicles. They had arrived, driving with masked head-lights, during the night of June 19–20. During the day they lay silent. They must not make a sound. At the mere rattle of a hatch cover the troop commanders would have fits. Only when dusk fell were they allowed to go to the stream in the clearing to wash themselves, a troop at a time.

"The regiment was bivouacking in the forest in full battle order. Each tank, moreover, carried ten jerricans of petrol strapped to its turret and had a trailer in tow with a further three drums. These were the preparations for a long journey, not a swift battle. 'You don't go into battle with jerricans on your tank,' the experienced tankmen were saying.

"A fantastic rumour swept through the field kitchens. 'Stalin has leased the Ukraine to Hitler and we're just going to occupy it.' "

Hitler himself had had his command post carefully concealed. "This great H.Q.," recalls Paul Schmidt, "was hidden in a thick forest near Rastenburg in East Prussia. One recalled the old tales of witches. Not without reason was the H.Q. known by the code-name of *Wolfsschanze* (Wolf's lair).

"The atmosphere of the post in the dark Prussian forest was depressing for people coming from sunnier parts.

"The rooms were tiny. You always felt constricted. The humidity which came from masses of concrete, the permanent electric light, the constant hum of the air-conditioning imposed an air of unreality on the atmosphere in which Hitler, growing paler and more flabby every day, received the foreign visitors. The whole place might easily have been the mystic retreat of some legendary spirit of evil."

Nevertheless, since the coming of spring, London, Vichy, Berne, Stockholm, Tokyo, and Washington had been expecting a decisive split between the signatories of the German-Soviet Non-Aggression Pact of August 23, 1939, and were already calculating the effect this immense extension of the war would have.

Only the Kremlin refused until the last moment to admit that Hitler was about to cross his Rubicon. Stalin took none of the measures which were clearly required if Russia was to be prepared for the imminent change in the political and military situation. The *Great Patriotic War* explains his strange blindness in this way:

"One of the reasons for the error made in the appreciation of the situation is that J. V. Stalin, who alone decided the most important political and military questions, was of the opinion that Germany would not break the Non-Aggression Pact in the near future. Therefore he considered all the reports of German troop movements merely as evidence of provocations, intended to force the Soviet Union into counter-measures.

"If he took such measures, Stalin feared he might furnish the Hitlerian clique with a good pretext for accusing the U.S.S.R. of having broken the treaty and attacking Germany treacherously. For the same reasons, certain commanders of military districts who wanted to place their troops in defensive positions and have them ready for combat, had their requests refused.

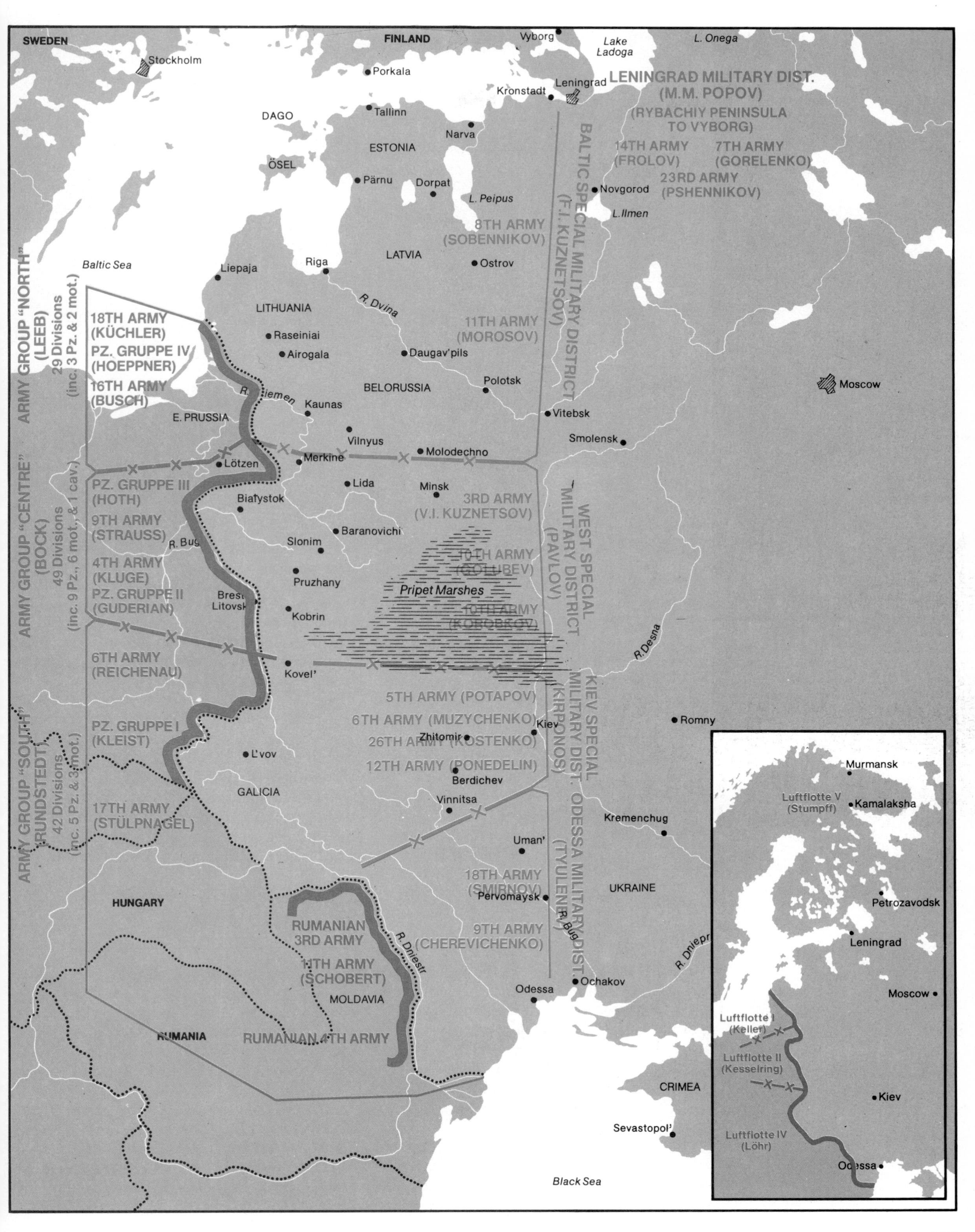
SWEDEN
FINLAND
Stockholm
Porkala
Vyborg
Lake Ladoga
L. Onega
Kronstadt
Leningrad
LENINGRAD MILITARY DIST.
(M.M. POPOV)
(RYBACHIY PENINSULA TO VYBORG)
14TH ARMY (FROLOV)
7TH ARMY (GORELENKO)
23RD ARMY (PSHENNIKOV)
DAGO
Tallinn
Narva
ESTONIA
ÖSEL
Pärnu
Dorpat
L. Peipus
Novgorod
L. Ilmen
BALTIC SPECIAL MILITARY DISTRICT (F.I. KUZNETSOV)
8TH ARMY (SOBENNIKOV)
Baltic Sea
Liepaja
Riga
LATVIA
Ostrov
R. Dvina
LITHUANIA
11TH ARMY (MOROSOV)
ARMY GROUP "NORTH" (LEEB)
29 Divisions (inc. 3 Pz. & 2 mot.)
18TH ARMY (KÜCHLER)
PZ. GRUPPE IV (HOEPPNER)
16TH ARMY (BUSCH)
Raseiniai
Airogala
Daugav'pils
Polotsk
Moscow
BELORUSSIA
Kaunas
E. PRUSSIA
Vitebsk
Vilnyus
Smolensk
Molodechno
Merkine
Lötzen
ARMY GROUP "CENTRE" (BOCK)
49 Divisions (inc. 9 Pz., 6 mot., & 1 cav.)
PZ. GRUPPE III (HOTH)
9TH ARMY (STRAUSS)
4TH ARMY (KLUGE)
PZ. GRUPPE II (GUDERIAN)
Lida
Minsk
Białystok
3RD ARMY (V.I. KUZNETSOV)
WEST SPECIAL MILITARY DISTRICT (PAVLOV)
Baranovichi
Slonim
R. Bug
10TH ARMY (GOLUBEV)
Pruzhany
Pripet Marshes
Brest Litovsk
Kobrin
10TH ARMY (KOROBKOV)
R. Desna
6TH ARMY (REICHENAU)
Kovel'
5TH ARMY (POTAPOV)
6TH ARMY (MUZYCHENKO)
26TH ARMY (KOSTENKO)
12TH ARMY (PONEDELIN)
KIEV SPECIAL MILITARY DIST. (KIRPONOS)
Kiev
Zhitomir
Romny
Berdichev
ARMY GROUP "SOUTH" (RUNDSTEDT)
42 Divisions (inc. 5 Pz. & 3 mot.)
PZ. GRUPPE I (KLEIST)
17TH ARMY (STÜLPNAGEL)
L'vov
GALICIA
Vinnitsa
Kremenchug
Uman'
ODESSA MILITARY DIST. (TYULENEV)
18TH ARMY (SMIRNOV)
Pervomaysk
UKRAINE
R. Bug
HUNGARY
RUMANIAN 3RD ARMY
R. Dniestr
9TH ARMY (CHEREVICHENKO)
R. Dniepr
11TH ARMY (SCHOBERT)
MOLDAVIA
Odessa
Ochakov
RUMANIA
RUMANIAN 4TH ARMY
CRIMEA
Sevastopol'
Black Sea
Murmansk
Luftflotte V (Stumpff)
Kamalaksha
Petrozavodsk
Leningrad
Moscow
Luftflotte I (Keller)
Luftflotte II (Kesselring)
Kiev
Luftflotte IV (Löhr)
Odessa

▲ *Indicative of how Stalin's massive purges carved the brains out of the Red Army. Only one of the Marshals in this photograph survived. All the others were ruthlessly weeded out and either killed or imprisoned.* Top row, left to right: *Army Commissar First Rank Gamarnik; Marshal Tukachevsky (creator of the Red Army's tank force); Marshal Yegorov; General Hapepsky; Admiral Orlov; General Yakir.* Bottom row, left to right: *General Kamenev, Commissar Ordzhonikidze; Marshal Budenny; General Alksnis; Commissar Muklevich; General Eideman; General Uborevich. Budenny was the sole survivor of this group.*

"The People's Defence Commissar, Marshal of the Soviet Union Timoshenko, and G. K. Zhukov, Chief-of-Staff, bear a heavy burden of responsibility for the unpreparedness of the Red Army to resist a surprise attack. They had not appreciated the military and political situation clearly enough and had not understood that immediate measures to put the armed forces into combat readiness were essential."

Churchill warns Stalin

There is nothing surprising in Stalin's refusal to believe Churchill's warning about an imminent German attack. The message that the British Prime Minister sent him on April 3 and which, for various reasons, was not handed him until the 22nd was not explicit enough to have made him change his views:

"*Prime Minister to Sir Stafford Cripps* [British Ambassador in Moscow]

"Following from me to M. Stalin, *provided it can be personally delivered by you:*

"I have sure information from a trusted agent that when the Germans thought they had got Yugoslavia in the net–that is to say, after March 20–they began to move three out of the five Panzer divisions from Roumania to southern Poland. The moment they heard of the Serbian revolution this movement was countermanded. Your Excellency will readily appreciate the significance of these facts."

Stalin did nothing, fearing that Churchill, using all kinds of forged information, was trying to create a split between Berlin and Moscow and to divert the weight of German arms from Great Britain to the Soviet Union. Though history has shown these suspicions to be groundless, the man in the Kremlin cannot be blamed for being on his guard.

Soviet spies at work

The fact remains, however, that the British message of April 3 was soon corroborated by a deluge of information which ought to have found more credence in Moscow, since it originated from Soviet spy networks in the Far East and Central Europe.

At the outbreak of war the *Frankfurter Zeitung*'s Far East correspondent, Richard Sorge, long in the pay of the Soviet Secret Service, had been sent as Press Attaché to the German Embassy in Tokyo. General Eugen Ott, Hitler's envoy to the Mikado, was well connected in Japanese circles and kept no secrets from Sorge.

So, on May 19, this informer, an old hand at his calling and particularly well placed, reported the concentration of nine armies (which was correct) and 150 German divisions (he underestimated by three) facing the Soviet frontiers. On June 1, he described the strategy the Nazis would use; and on June 15, he gave June 22 as the date of attack. "Too good to be true," it might have been thought, when the first revelations of Richard Sorge's exploits appeared some 20 years ago. The fact that in 1964 the Kremlin awarded him posthumously the title of "Hero of the Soviet Union" and issued a commemorative postage stamp, indicates the importance of his services to Russia.

The "Lucy Ring"

In Switzerland there was a network known to the *Abwehr* as the "Red Trio" (or "Lucy Ring") because of the three clandestine transmitters which it used to communicate from Lausanne and Geneva.

The three "musicians", as they were known in Moscow, were led by the German Rudolf Rössler, known under the codename "Lucy", a German refugee of Christian Progressive hue who lived, ostensibly, as a bookseller in Lucerne. Where did this agent obtain the information that he communicated to Moscow? Even today this question is difficult to answer. From the value of the information he gathered and the three or four days he took to obtain it each time, it is reasonable to conclude that he got it from someone who took part in the most secret conferences of O.K.W.

A proof of this, in respect of Operation "Barbarossa", is the description of Rössler's information given by General Otto Heilbrunn in the book he wrote about the Soviet Secret Service. "Not only had the 'Red Trio' given the date of the attack to its Moscow control, but it had also supplied the German plan of campaign, the composition and numbers of Army Groups "North", "Centre", and "South", with precise details of the number of tanks and their distribution between the groups. What is more, Moscow now knew the intentions of the enemy, his directions of attack, and his precise objectives. Lastly Moscow was told the names of all senior officers down to the corps commanders."

Never had a state been better informed than Russia about the aggressive intent of another. Never had the accuracy of the information been so highly guaranteed, since there could have been no collusion between Sorge and Rössler. But never had an army been so ill-prepared to meet the initial onslaught of its enemy than the Red Army on June 22, 1941.

Soviet forces were dispersed too widely

With 138 infantry divisions and 40 motorised and armoured divisions under arms between the frozen Arctic Ocean and the Danube delta, the Red Army could have been expected to hold the attack of some 200 German and satellite divisions, had it been properly deployed for a defensive campaign. But it was not. The troops of the Baltic Special Military District were dispersed between the Niemen and the Dvina to a depth of nearly 200 miles. It

▽ *Bed-rock of the Red Army: the infantry masses, forced to stand up to the Wehrmacht professionals with only indifferent leadership and with little but their own courage to absorb the shock of "Barbarossa".*

▵ *June 22, 1941: Ribbentrop formally announces the invasion of Russia to the press, hours after the actual attack had gone in. "When Barbarossa begins the world will hold its breath and make no comment," Hitler boasted. He was wrong on one count. The assault on Russia provoked an immediate declaration of alliance from Churchill, who for decades had been as outspoken a critic of Communism as Hitler himself. "If Hitler invaded Hell," Churchill commented, "I should at least make a favourable reference to the Devil in the House of Commons."*
▹ *H-Hour on the Eastern Front: German troops prepare to attack.*

was worse in the West Special Military District where General Pavlov had placed divisions along the whole 300 mile line between Białystok and Minsk. The situation was slightly better, though still not satisfactory, in the Kiev District.

This dispersal of Soviet Forces was the pattern the length of the German-Russian demarcation line. There is no getting away from the fact that the fronts were too long for the divisions detailed to garrison them. For instance, according to the *Great Patriotic War*, the Russians had only the 125th Division covering a 25-mile front facing *Panzergruppe* IV which, on June 22, put two infantry divisions and three armoured divisions into the field. The situation was the same in the sectors awaiting the onslaught of Hoth and Guderian, powerfully supported by Colonel-General von Richthofen's Stukas.

One June 18, a German deserter crossed into the Russian lines near Kovel' and reported the attack as coming on June 22. But this extra proof provoked no greater reaction from the Kremlin than the information it had previously received. Nevertheless, on the night of June 21, after midnight, the penny dropped and at 0030 hours the commanders of the military districts concerned were ordered to occupy their front line positions, disperse and camouflage their aircraft, and put the A.A. on full alert. But they were not to take "any other steps without special orders". This instruction, however, insufficient as it was, had not reached all commanders before they found themselves at grips with forces which were very much greater in numbers and in armament. Furthermore, the Russian communications with the rear had been cut by the German artillery bombardment, which began at 0335 hours that morning and destroyed the Russian telephone networks. At 0415 the barrage of shells was followed by the wide-ranging destruction of Russian barbed wire by German sappers. The Stukas, diving from high in the sky, alternated with the artillery in pounding the bewildered Soviet Union.

The war had come to Russia.

CHAPTER 40

BARBAROSSA: the clash

On the evening of June 22, in the headquarters which German G.H.Q. had just taken over at Lötzen in East Prussia, Halder observed in his invaluable diary:

"The enemy has been taken unawares by our attack. His forces were not tactically in position for defence. In the frontier zone his troops were widely dispersed and his frontier defence was weak overall.

"Because of our tactical surprise, enemy resistance on the frontier has been weak and disorganised. We have been able to seize bridges over the border rivers and, slightly further on, to overwhelm enemy positions fortified by deep earthworks."

Stalin's failure to react until the very eve of the German attack is astonishing. Some validity can be given to the explanation given by one of the best-informed biographers of the Russian leader:

"At dawn on June 22, 1941," writes Emmanuel d'Astier de la Vigerie, "on the day before the anniversary of Napoleon's crossing of the Niemen, 120 divisions speed towards Kiev, Leningrad, and Moscow, where the theatre is performing *A Midsummer Night's Dream.*

"Stalin, living in a dream world of hope, has spurned warnings and refused advice. During the first hours of the attack he issued orders that German firing is not to be answered. He would like to think he is faced by nothing more than a provocative act from a few ill-disciplined German units. On June 21, a German Communist worker deserted and revealed the date and time of the attack. Stalin is told but refuses to believe the evidence. Fifteen years later Nikita Khruschev recounts the episode; and another historian adds that Stalin ordered Korpik, the deserting worker, who could in his view only be an *agent provocateur*, to be shot."

Soviet resistance in chaos

To the north of the Pripet Marshes, Soviet resistance had, from the early hours of that warm summer morning, been surprised and overcome more or less everywhere. The same fate had overcome reinforcements moving up to the front to obey People's Defence Commissar Marshal Timoshenko's broadcast message of 0715 hours:

"Our troops must hurl themselves with

▽ Field-Marshal Fedor von Bock, commander of Army Group "Centre", the strongest of the three army groups, whose task it was to destroy the Soviet armoured and motorised forces in the triangle Vilnyus–Smolensk–Brest.

▷ Safe from air attack, German trucks and dispatch riders wait in a traffic jam on the borders of the Soviet Union.

▲ *German troops double towards a burning farm house. Resistance on the frontier was disorganised and weak, but following Stalin's speech of July 3 the defence stiffened and the "scorched earth" policy was carried out ruthlessly.*

all their means and energy against the enemy and annihilate them in all places where they have violated our frontiers."

In Army Group "Centre's" area, Colonel-General Guderian had taken the bridges over the River Bug, above and below Brest-Litovsk, by storm, and by the evening his XXIV Panzer Corps (General Geyr von Schweppenburg) was in Kobrin and his XLVII Panzer Corps (General Lemelsen) in Pruzhany, 41 and 47 miles respectively from their jump-off points.

This enormous success by *Panzergruppe* II was equalled and even surpassed by that of *Panzergruppe* III. Not only had Colonel-General Hoth penetrated deeply into the Russian defences but his LVII Panzer Corps (General Kuntzen) and his XXXIX Panzer Corps (General R. Schmidt) had taken the bridges over the Niemen at Merkine and Olyta intact. The XXXIX Corps was in fact 59 miles over the demarcation line.

This ultra-rapid war of movement led at times to comic incidents such as this adventure of General Guderian:

"I next visited the front line in Slonim and then drove in a Panzer IV through no-man's-land to the 18th Panzer Division. At 15.30 hrs I was back in Slonim having ordered the 18th Panzer Division to push on in the direction of Baranovichi, while the 29th (Motorised) Infantry Division was instructed to hasten its advance towards Slonim. I then returned to my Group command post. This drive took me unexpectedly through the middle of Russian infantry, which had come up in lorries to the very outskirts of Slonim and was on the point of dismounting. I ordered my driver, who was next to me, to go full speed ahead and we drove straight through the Russians; they were so surprised by this unexpected encounter that they did not even have time to fire their guns. All the same they must have recognised me because the Russian press later announced my death; I felt bound to inform them of their mistake by means of the German wireless."

In Army Group "North", Field-Marshal von Leeb had no reason to be any less satisfied with the results of the first day of the campaign. *Panzergruppe* IV (Colonel-General Hoeppner) had also thrown the Russians into disorder; in particular, at about 1900 hours, the LVI Panzer Corps (General von Manstein) had boldly seized the important viaduct which crosses the Doubissa gorges at Airogala. He was about 50 miles from his starting point.

As for the Soviet Air Force, those planes

▷ *The attack rolls east. The German Army relied heavily on horses and requisitioned and captured transport, though French trucks and tanks were not sufficiently robust for the appalling road conditions.*
▽ *Soldiers take a hand at pushing a cart out of the dusty rutted tracks that were called roads in Russia.*

▷ *Mixed transport moves through a typical Russian village with its wooden houses and dusty road.*

which had not been destroyed on the ground in the first hour made a rather pitiful impression on General Kesselring:

"From the second day onward I watched the battle against the aircraft which were arriving from the depths of Russia. It seemed almost criminal to me that they should use formations which were so ridiculous from the point of view of aerial tactics, and machines obviously incapable of getting out of trouble in the air. In they came, one squadron after the other, at regular intervals, and one after the other they crashed, easy prey to our fighters. 'This is the massacre of the innocents,' I thought. So completely did we manage to crush the basis of any future bomber fleet that Russian bombers never appeared again throughout the whole campaign!"

In contrast, south of the Pripet Marshes, the achievements of Field-Marshal von Rundstedt had been no greater than what German military theorists call an "ordinary victory", and it had not been possible to split off units from *Panzergruppe* I (Colonel-General von Kleist) to exploit the success.

The designs of the Third Reich on the Ukraine were known to all and so Stalin had emphasised the defence of the approaches to that territory. It was defended by 68 divisions, including ten armoured and five motorised, while Rundstedt had only 54 divisions under him, including 12 Rumanian, five Panzer, and three motorised divisions. Furthermore, following an order from Hitler, the German 11th Army (seven divisions), which had been concentrated in Moldavia, did not join battle on June 22. This allowed the Russians to assemble part of the forces they had aligned along the Rumanian frontier and use them profitably in Galicia.

The performance of Soviet officers and men

Looking at the Soviet Army and the performance of its officers and men, the testimony of General Fedyuninsky, who was fighting in Kovel' that day, may be useful. As his memoirs have not been translated into any Western language, they will be quoted in the translation given by Alexander Werth:

"Railway junctions and lines of communication were being destroyed by German planes and diversionist groups. There was a shortage of wireless sets at army headquarters, nor did any of us know how to use them . . . Orders and instructions were slow in arriving, and sometimes did not arrive at all . . . The liaison with the neighbouring units was often completely absent, while nobody tried to establish it. Taking advantage of this, the enemy would often penetrate into our rear, and attack the Soviet headquarters . . . Despite German air supremacy, our marching columns did not use any proper camouflage. Sometimes on narrow roads, bottlenecks were formed by troops, artillery, motor vehicles, and field kitchens, and then the Nazi planes had the time of their life." In such conditions the higher levels of the front line command often performed rather poorly. Certain commanders, such as General Boldin, performed heroically; he managed to blast his way through the German lines with 2,000 men of his XIII Corps; others, such as General D. G. Pavlov, who was shot, together with his chief-of-staff and General Korobkov of the 10th Army, lost their heads. Opposite *Panzergruppe* III a Lithuanian division went over to the Germans and, as Fedyuninsky points out, at first cannon shot many Ukrainian partisans rebelled against their September 1939 "liberators". In contrast, the Brest-Litovsk garrison, surrounded on the evening of June 22, held out to July 24, under a hail of bombs and artillery fire, among which were monster 2.2-ton shells

▽ *Crouching in a shell hole an N.C.O. of the* Waffen-S.S. *primes his hand grenade before going in to mop up a party of Russians. Well supplied with modern equipment, the S.S. came to serve as a "fire brigade" on the Eastern Front, blocking counter-attacks and heading offensives.*

K
10

fired by the 61.5-cm mortar *Karl*.

In many other sectors, once he had overcome his initial shock, the Russian soldier fought with a stubbornness and bravery admitted by most German combatants who have written about the campaign:

"The Russians again proved their mastery in forest fighting. With sure instinct they moved among the impenetrable undergrowth. Their positions, not on the forest's edge but deep inside, were superbly camouflaged. Their dugouts and foxholes were established with diabolical cunning, providing a field of fire only to the rear. From the front and from above they were invisible. The German infantrymen passed them unsuspecting, and were picked off from behind.

"The Russians were also very good at infiltrating into enemy positions. Moving singly, they communicated with each other in the dense forest by imitating the cries of animals, and after trickling through the German positions they rallied again and reformed as assault units. The headquarters staff of 247th Infantry Regiment fell victim to these Russian tactics.

"In the night, at 0200, the shout went up, 'Action Stations!' There was small-arms

The Panzers drive east. The wear on men and machines became a considerable problem with the huge distances and almost non-existent roads.
△ *Tanks of* Panzergruppe *Kleist spread out either side of a dust track that would disolve into a mud bath by autumn.*
◁ ◁ *A Pzkw III fords one of the many rivers which formed natural obstacles for attackers on the Eastern Front.*
◁ *Dispatch riders slump exhausted over their battered machines.*

fire. The Russians were outside the regimental head-quarters. They had surrounded it. With fixed bayonets they broke into the officers' quarters. The regimental adjutant, the orderly officer, and the regimental medical officer were cut down in the doorway of their forest ranger's hut. N.C.O.s and headquarters personnel were killed before they could reach their pistols or carbines.

"Lieutenant-Colonel Brehmer, the regimental commander, succeeded in barricading himself behind a woodpile and defending himself throughout two hours with his sub-machine-gun."

In Moscow, on June 22, the Praesidium of the Supreme Soviet announced the mobilisation of the reserves of the years 1925 to 1938, thus recalling 15 million men to the colours. The next day, Supreme Headquarters began work. Stalin, assisted by Molotov, took control. General Zhukov, and later General Shaposhnikov, served as Chiefs-of-Staff. Marshals Voroshilov, Timoshenko, and Budenny played their parts until they were called to direct field operations, Voroshilov in the Baltic countries, Timoshenko in Belorussia, and Budenny in the Ukraine. In their new posts they enjoyed the services of Comrades Zhdanov, Bulganin, and Khruschev as political advisers.

Timoshenko gave up his position as People's Defence Commissar and was succeeded by Stalin who, on August 7, had himself appointed to the post of Supreme Commander of the Soviet Armed Forces.

The general running of the war fell to the National Defence Committee. This was presided over by Stalin, and its members were Molotov, Voroshilov, Malenkov, and the sinister L. P. Beria in his capacity as head of the Soviet Secret Service or N.K.V.D.

On July 3, 1941, Stalin broadcast:

"Comrades, citizens, brothers and sisters, men of our Army and Navy! I speak to you, my friends!"

This sort of language from the tongue of the cruel master of the "purges" of previous years was unfamiliar, but nevertheless, as Alexander Werth has pointed out, it evoked an enormous response.

"A serious threat hangs over our country," he went on. "It can only be dispersed by the combined efforts of the military and industrial might of the nation. There is no room for the timid or the coward, for deserters or spreaders of panic, and a merciless struggle must be waged against such people. We must destroy spies, *agents provocateurs*, and enemy parachutists . . . On the spot court-martials will try anyone who, through panic or cowardice, hinders our defence, whatever his post or rank."

Stalin expressed himself in this way not only because he had to consider a possible Fifth Column, but also because he was hinting at anybody who might have been tempted to ask him to justify his policies over the previous two years. Whatever his intentions, he gave the order that, if the enemy push became stronger, the Russians should abandon only "scorched earth" to the invader:

▽ German soldiers from Army Group "Centre" pass a dump of vehicles abandoned by the Soviet 3rd, 4th, and 10th Armies. Later, as the tide of war turned against them, the Germans began to make more and more use of the vast stocks of captured Russian vehicles and artillery in both East and West.
△ ▷ After blasting them from cover, the crew of a 10.5-cm gun howitzer take on the Russian defenders of Zhitomir with rifle fire. The combination of infantry and artillery was typical of the savage, close-quarter street fighting that culminated in the Battle of Stalingrad.
▽ ▷ A pitiful collection of furniture stands outside the houses of a Russian town caught up in the Germans' swift advance. But fast though it was, the Russian "scorched earth" policy was to deprive the Germans of the supplies and shelter they were to need so badly in the coming winter.

▵ ▵ *Yet another jibe at the legendary "Russian steamroller", this time by Lino Palacio of Argentina's* La Razón – *"Comrade, we're out of steam."*
▵ *Karl Arnold of* Simplicissimus, *Munich, depicts a rapidly-retreating Stalin gasping "The world revolution is on the march!"*

"The enemy must not find a single railway-engine, not a wagon, not a pound of bread or a glassful of petrol. All the *Kolkhozes* [collective farms] must bring in their herds and hand their stocks of wheat over to official bodies to be sent to the rear. Everything that is usable but cannot be sent back (such as wheat, petrol, or non-ferrous metals) must be destroyed."

Lastly, he decreed the setting-up of partisan units which would take the war into the enemy rearguard and destroy his communications.

There was also a change in military organisation. The corps (the formation between the army and the division) was abandoned and, as already mentioned, the armoured, motorised, and mechanised brigades were no longer to be formed into divisions. Furthermore, infantry divisions were required to give up one of their artillery regiments. This enabled Russian G.H.Q. to organise large artillery units as the High Command's reserve of firepower.

The Germans reach the Black Sea

However, before these various measures had had time to produce the desired effect, the situation between the Black Sea and the Baltic had developed at frightening speed, to the disadvantage and dismay of the Russians.

From the Black Sea to the Pripet Marshes, Army Group "South" had finally overcome Soviet resistance. L'vov fell on June 30 and on July 2, the German 11th Army, which included the Rumanian 3rd Army (General Dumitrescu), went over to the attack. Three days later, the German 6th Army (Field-Marshal von Reichenau) succeeded in punching a hole through the fortified positions constructed by the Russians near the old Polish-Soviet frontier; *Panzergruppe* I drove into the breach along the Berdichev-Zhitomir line and it is possible that its III Panzer Corps (General von Mackensen) would have taken Kiev and the Dniepr bridges if a sudden order from Hitler had not forbidden him to risk his tanks in this large city.

He was forced to wait outside Kiev to be replaced by the German 6th Army, and then wheel from the east to the south-east. On August 2, near Pervomaysk, on the Bug, the 6th Army linked forces with

▹ *July 16: German soldiers, with Russian prisoners carrying their ammunition boxes, move down to the Dniepr. It was on this river line that Rundstedt recommended that the German Army should wait for spring before attempting the final assault on Moscow in 1942.*

△ In the wake of the Panzers come the infantry. Headed by their N.C.O.s, a column of German infantry crosses a newly-constructed bridge. Though it was the Panzers that made the breakthroughs, it was the infantry who had the job of grinding down the pockets of Russian resistance after the battles of encirclement.
▷ German grenadiers crouch behind their 3.7-cm anti-tank gun as Russian transport burns in the background. At the beginning of the Russian campaign, the 3.7-cm gun was being replaced as the standard divisional anti-tank gun by the new 5-cm weapon. The Russians, on the other hand, though possessing a larger number of tanks than the Germans, were definitely inferior in anti-tank guns, having only 48 45-mm guns per division, compared with the Germans' 72 3.7-cm or 5-cm guns.

Colonel-General von Stülpnagel's 17th Army, which had arrived after forced marches from Vinnitsa. The Soviet 6th, 12th, and part of the 18th Armies had their lines of retreat cut off and were wiped out. The victors captured 103,000 prisoners, 317 tanks, and 858 guns, all that remained of seven corps (22 divisions). Rapidly exploiting their success, the Germans reached the Black Sea near Ochakov.

Army Group "Centre" takes 328,000 prisoners

This success was notable but not as remarkable as that of Field-Marshal von Bock. By June 25, Guderian had arrived at Baranovichi and Hoth had reached Lida and Molodechno, both more than 125 miles east of Białystok, where the unfortunate Pavlov was still bottled up. On the next day the two *Gruppen* established first contact at Slonim, and at Minsk on the 29th the pincers closed behind the Russians, who had left the decision to retreat until too late. On July 8, according to Halder's diary, of the 43 divisions in the Soviet 3rd, 4th, 10th Armies, 32 could be taken as annihilated. The Germans counted close on 290,000 prisoners, as well as 2,585 tanks, 1,449 guns, and 246 aircraft captured or destroyed.

A second pincer movement was closed at Smolensk on July 16, when *Panzergruppe* II, which had advanced to Elnia after forcing the bridges over the Berezina and the Dniepr, met *Panzergruppe* III, which had sped from Polotsk to Vitebsk and then wheeled south to meet Guderian. Here O.K.H. amalgamated the two *Gruppen* as the 4th *Panzerarmee* (Tank Army), with Kluge as its commander.

Unfortunately, Kluge could not get on with his impetuous subordinates, who accused him of failing to understand the tactical possibilities of tanks and restricting their initiative to an intolerable degree. Whatever the effect of this friction, the Smolensk sector was the centre of a furious struggle until August 8. The Russians trapped in the pocket tried to break through the perimeter which hemmed them in. From outside, Timoshenko and Lieutenant-General A. I. Eremenko tried to break through to the besieged Russian forces.

In the final analysis, all was in vain.

△ *During a break in the fighting a German officer summons his N.C.O.s to the lee of a Pzkw III. When the fighting was going their way, German officers had a freedom of movement that would be lost with later "stand and fight" orders from Hitler.*
◁ *A Pzkw III drives past a burning BT-7. Of the 29 Russian armoured divisions, 20 had been practically eliminated by the beginning of July.*

▷ *Russian peasants watch as a half-track tows a 15-cm gun. Besides being hampered by bad roads, the Germans were worn out by the enormous distances that they had to cover on the Eastern Front.*
▷ ▷ *Covered by a light anti-aircraft gun, German engineers rebuild a demolished bridge.*
▽ ▷ *An officer of the Luftwaffe* Flak *artillery cuts himself a trophy from a downed Soviet bomber.*

▽ *A horse-drawn supply column in difficulties at a ford. Rivers that were streams in summer would become torrents in the autumn rains. Some authorities believe that the Germans could have defeated Russia in the time-table they had set themselves if there had been a system of modern roads and bridges as in France and western Europe.*

△ *Pioneers operate a ferry with two inflatable assault boats, while engineers examine a demolished trestle bridge.*

Marshal Timoshenko was defeated at Roslavl' and Guderian took 38,000 prisoners, 300 tanks, and 300 guns. When fighting ceased in the "cauldron" of Smolensk, a communiqué from O.K.H. announced the capture of 310,000 prisoners and the capture or destruction of more than 3,000 armoured vehicles and 3,000 pieces of artillery. At Elnia, the Panzers were 200 miles from Moscow but, since June 22, they had travelled 440 miles, mostly on unmetalled roads, in dust which had scored their pistons and cylinders mercilessly.

The Gulf of Riga occupied

In Army Group "North", *Panzergruppe* IV was counter-attacked strongly near Raseiniai on June 24 by the Soviet XII Armoured Corps, which launched 100 immense KV-1 tanks against the Germans. Even so, the Russians were cut to pieces and this success allowed LVI Panzer Corps to take Daugav'pils during the course of 26th without the Russians having time to destroy the bridges over the Dvina. Kaunas and Vilnyus fell to the 16th Army, Liepaja and Riga to the 18th. The Lithuanians and Letts welcomed the Germans as liberators, but Hitler had no intention of restoring their independence

Beginning his push on July 2, Hoeppner reassembled his *Panzergruppe* on the right bank of the Dvina, moved up to the fortified Russo-Latvian frontier and forced it at Ostrov, opening the way for his XLI Panzer Corps (General Reinhardt) to capture the important centre of Pskov on the eastern shore of Lake Peipus on July 8, and his comrade Manstein to manoeuvre in the direction of Novgorod. Meanwhile, the 16th Army had established links with the 9th Army (Army Group "Centre") near Vitebsk and the 18th had established itself along a line from Lake Peipus, through Dorpat, to Pärnu on the Gulf of Riga.

From now on, the operations of Army Group "North" would slow down markedly, because of Soviet resistance and counter-attacks and also as a result of the swampy nature of the area and the heavy rain. Another reason was that Leeb had given different objectives to his *Panzergruppe* IV. Its LVI Panzer Corps was to drive on Novgorod while its XLI Panzer Corps moved towards Narva.

Halder surveys the results

Though not everything had gone according to plan during this first phase of the campaign, the German Chief-of-Staff was nevertheless satisfied with the results that had been achieved. On July 3, he wrote in his diary:

"All in all, I can already say that we have carried out the task entrusted to us, which was to crush the mass of the Russian Army between the Dvina and the Dniepr rivers."

On July 8 his optimism was confirmed by the figures of Russian losses that were submitted to him:

"Of the 164 infantry divisions which the Red Army mobilised, 89 have been completely or partially destroyed. Forty-six Russian divisions are still fighting and in reasonable condition. Eighteen are in other sectors (14 in Finland and four in the Caucasus) and a maximum of 11 are in reserve in the interior of the Soviet Union. Of the 29 armoured divisions mobilised, 20 have been completely or partially destroyed and nine are still fully fit for combat. The Russians can no longer offer a continuous front even using the best defensive positions."

In spite of the hecatombs of Minsk,

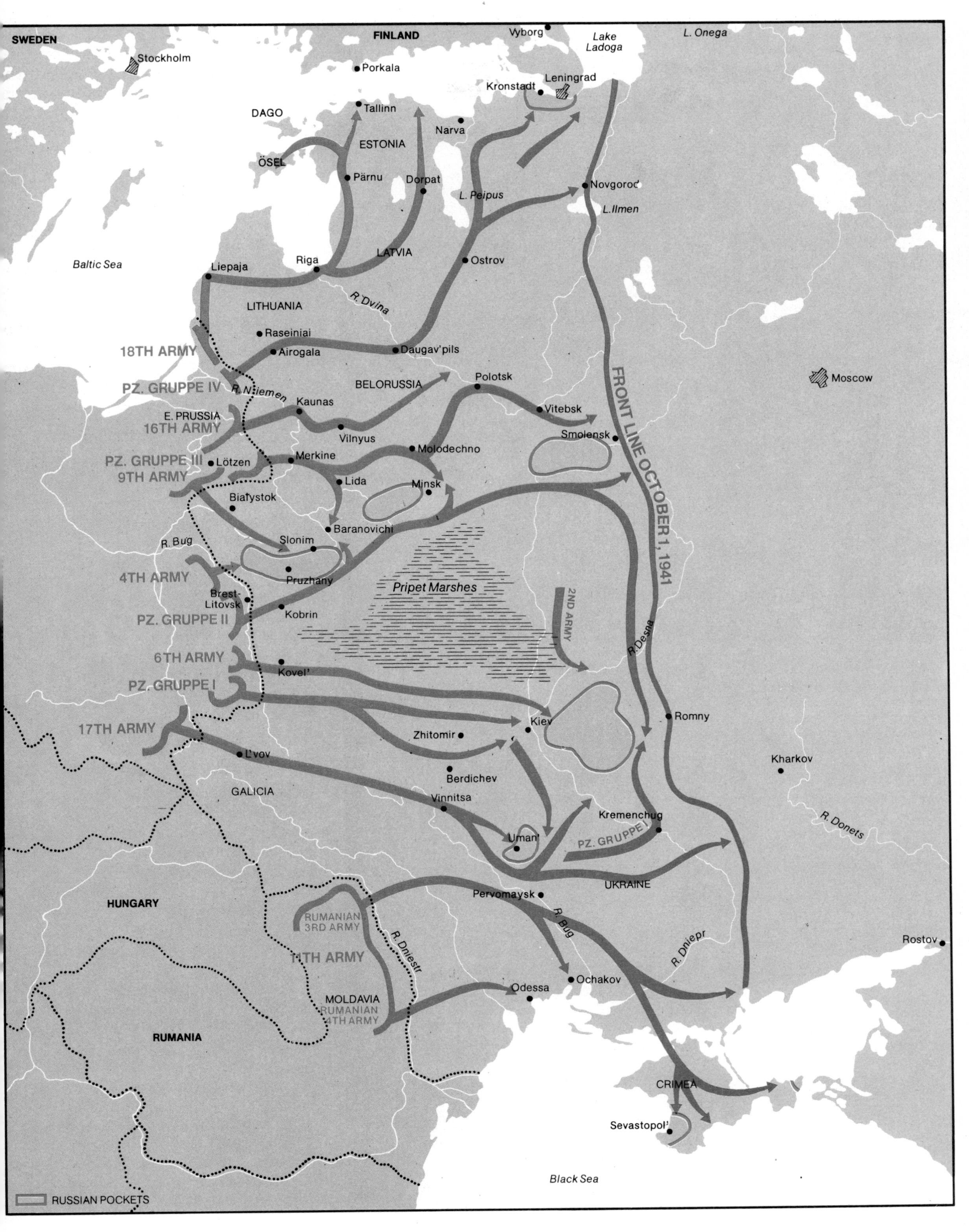
SWEDEN
FINLAND
Vyborg
Lake Ladoga
L. Onega
Stockholm
Porkala
Leningrad
Kronstadt
Tallinn
DAGO
Narva
ESTONIA
ÖSEL
Pärnu
Dorpat
L. Peipus
Novgorod
L.Ilmen
Baltic Sea
LATVIA
Riga
Liepaja
Ostrov
R. Dvina
LITHUANIA
Raseiniai
18TH ARMY
Airogala
Daugav'pils
PZ. GRUPPE IV
R. Niemen
BELORUSSIA
Polotsk
Moscow
FRONT LINE OCTOBER 1, 1941
E. PRUSSIA
Kaunas
16TH ARMY
Vilnyus
Vitebsk
Smolensk
Molodechno
PZ. GRUPPE III
Lötzen
Merkine
9TH ARMY
Lida
Minsk
Białystok
Baranovichi
R. Bug
Slonim
4TH ARMY
Pruzhany
Pripet Marshes
2ND ARMY
Brest-Litovsk
Kobrin
PZ. GRUPPE II
R.Desna
6TH ARMY
Kovel'
PZ. GRUPPE I
Romny
17TH ARMY
Kiev
Zhitomir
L'vov
Kharkov
Berdichev
GALICIA
Vinnitsa
R. Donets
Kremenchug
Uman'
PZ. GRUPPE I
UKRAINE
Pervomaysk
HUNGARY
RUMANIAN 3RD ARMY
R. Bug
R. Dniestr
R. Dniepr
Rostov
11TH ARMY
Ochakov
Odessa
MOLDAVIA
RUMANIAN 4TH ARMY
RUMANIA
CRIMEA
Sevastopol'
Black Sea
RUSSIAN POCKETS

Białystok, Uman', and Smolensk, it is true that, on August 8, O.K.H. had identified 143 Russian divisions arrayed against the 136 German divisions, but many of them existed in name and number only. By August 13, the 53rd day of the campaign, German losses had reached the total of 389,924 officers, N.C.O.'s, and men, of whom 98,600 had been posted killed or missing. Yet between September 1, 1939 and May 31, 1941, the Polish, Norwegian, French, North African, and Balkan campaigns had cost the Wehrmacht only 97,000 killed out of a total of 218,109 casualties.

The figures for the Russian campaign indicated losses of 11 per cent of the effectives engaged on June 22, 1941. However, this did not yet dishearten Colonel-General Halder, who wrote on August 8, after listing the figures given above and estimating that 70 of the 143 Russian divisions were still barring the invaders' road to Moscow:

"This confirms my original belief that 'North' (Leeb) has sufficient forces to carry out its task, that all forces in the 'Centre' (Bock) must concentrate to crush the main mass of the enemy and that 'South' (Rundstedt) is strong enough to carry out its mission with success. It might even be able to help 'Centre'."

△ Faces drawn with fatigue and shock-some of the 290,000 prisoners taken by Army Group "Centre" by July 8. Russian losses were so heavy that few Germans believed that they could continue the war.
▷ In some villages in the Ukraine German troops were welcomed as liberators, but the insane political concept of the "Slavic sub-human" denied the Germans the opportunity of tapping this good will.
▷ ▷ A German soldier hugs the ground during an artillery bombardment in the savage fighting for the cauldron of Smolensk.

CHAPTER 41
Moscow or Kiev?

Evidently, O.K.H. still held to its original plan of attack. Once the Smolensk salient and the zone to its rear had been taken, the German Army would dash towards Moscow, stopping for nothing. It would not do this for the sake of vain prestige but because along that axis it would have the best chance of destroying the principal Russian forces. Hitler did not, however, share these views and, in any case, did not remain faithful to the plan he had accepted the previous winter. This had been to take Smolensk first, then Leningrad, and finally Moscow.

Hitler makes his decision: Leningrad

Between July 19 and August 12, he expressed his thoughts in four directives. Finally he made his decision:

1. Army Group "Centre", which was now in a salient, would go over to the defensive temporarily, co-operating with Army Group "South" on its right and allow Army Group "North" to borrow from it as many units and resources as it needed for its task.
2. Army Group "South" would prevent the defeated Russians from establishing themselves on the left bank of the Dniepr and would gain control of the Crimea, which otherwise the Russians could use as an air base to attack the Rumanian oilfields. This group would also overrun the industrial basins of Khar'kov and the Donets.
3. Army Group "North" would continue its offensive in order to cut off Leningrad and link up with the Finnish Army.

This programme, definitely established in Directive No. 34 of August 12, 1941, changed Brauchitsch's and his Chief-of-Staff's dreams of an arrow pointing straight to the Soviet capital into an open fan with its southern end pointing towards Rostov and its northern tip towards Leningrad. Naturally, Hitler had not given up hope of launching his powerful Army Group "Centre" against Moscow – but only after Rundstedt and Leeb had attained their objectives in the south and in the north.

But would they? Was the year not too far gone already to tackle the decisive act of the campaign?

This argument was certainly important, but Hitler clung obstinately to his views.

A new order to O.K.H. on August 21 cut short any more discussion. It declared unequivocally:

"O.K.H.'s suggestions of August 18 concerning the conduct of operations on the Eastern Front do not correspond with my views. My orders are:

"1. The essential target to be achieved before winter is not the capture of Moscow but the conquest of the Crimea and the Donets coal and industrial basin together with the interruption of oil supplies from the Caucasus. In the north, Leningrad must be invested and German forces must link up with the Finns, etc . . ."

The order was accompanied by a note in which Brauchitsch was reproached for

◁ *Tanks and infantry on the edge of one of the vast tracts of forest in central Russia. It was here that whole units of Russian soldiers cut off from their armies fought on as partisans.*

Overleaf: *A surprise capture, three T-34's bogged down in a swamp. Normally, its wide tracks and powerful engine gave the T-34 a cross-country capability that outclassed any German vehicle of the period. The T-34 stands as one of the major weapons of the war in the east; its tough and well-sloped armour, coupled with a 76.2-mm gun, made it a very formidable opponent for the Panzers.*

▽ *A pontoon bridge being built under fire over the Berezina. German engineers were efficient bridge builders and when the war turned against them they proved as effective with their demolitions.*